The Story of the

NAVAL ACADEMY

MY
BOOK

C. Warren Smith, III
from
_____ and Jimmy   Jan. 14, 1963.

The Story of the
NAVAL ACADEMY

FELIX RIESENBERG, JR.

Illustrated by William M. Hutchinson

RANDOM HOUSE · NEW YORK

To Mother

To Warren Smith, III
From the Alexanders
January 14, 1963

Contents

Foreword

The United States Naval Academy exists solely to educate and train future officers for career service in the Fleet. In the accomplishment of this aim, there is quite naturally a certain amount of "training" in the specific field of marine science; but for the most part the emphasis is on basic education, in order that the young officer will have a firm foundation on which to build through further study and experience.

This philosophy is not new. In fact, it is one of the reasons which brought about the establishment of the Naval Academy in 1845. It was recognized even before then that leaders of men had to be more than mere technicians in a specialty such as navigation, ordnance or engineering; that effective leadership was based on a thorough understanding of human nature and a broad knowledge of one's profession.

Someone once said that the prime requisites for good leadership are knowledge and character, and of the two, character is the more important in the ratio of at least two to one. We, who are entrusted with the responsibility of producing the future officers for the Fleet, believe this emphatically to be true. Consequently, almost every phase of the Naval Academy's four-year course bears on some facet of the development of character in the individual. The time-honored precepts of trustworthiness, loyalty and the highest degree of personal integrity are woven intimately into the lives of each midshipman. This, then, is the foundation from which spring such men as Admirals King, Nimitz and Halsey, Howard Gilmore, "Butch" O'Hare and Dan Callaghan.

Mr. Riesenberg has done a fine job in tracing the birth and development of the Naval Academy from its raw beginning. Today, the United States Naval Academy carries on in the traditions established by John Paul Jones and James Lawrence, producing men who dedicate their lives to guard our shores and defend our country and its way of life.

W. R. SMEDBERG, III
Rear Admiral, U.S. Navy
Superintendent,
United States Naval Academy

April, 1958

Author's Note

My first contact with the Naval Academy came when my brother, William P. Riesenberg, entered as a member of the Class of 1938. Recent talks with Bill brought back strong memories of the days when he was a midshipman. Our association gave added meaning to some seventy-five books I read before going back to Annapolis in the winter of 1957-1958 to start this work.

I wish to express appreciation for many courtesies shown me at the Naval Academy when Rear Admiral William R. Smedberg, III, was Superintendent. My thanks to Captains Harold E. Baker, D. O. Lacy and Jacob J. Vandergrift, Jr., and—especially—to Commander Marcy M. Dupre, III, for his enthusiasm in the work. Among civilian members of the Academy faculty who gave me so much time were Professor Vernon Tate, Librarian, and Associate Professor Robert M. Langdon.

Rear Admiral E. M. Eller, Director of Naval History, kindly supplied me with biographical material, and Dr. John Lyman of the Hydrographic Office advised me on many points.

Outside the Navy circle I was given the greatest help by my friend Kenneth McConnell, a former seafarer. And various kinds of aid came from my neighbors Bernice and John Derr, Richard Glendinning, Irene and MacKinlay Kantor, Betty Service and Stan Windhorn.

A final note which may be an omen of good: this book was written in a little house once owned by Commander Roy de S. Horn, the officer who wrote the first two verses of "Navy Blue and Gold."

Sarasota, Florida   *Felix Riesenberg, Jr.*
1958

The Story of the

NAVAL ACADEMY

I

The Naval Academy Today

Thirty miles east of the Nation's capital, imposing white buildings look out on the mouth of the Severn River at Annapolis, Maryland. Here is the United States Naval Academy where midshipmen are in training four years to become officers in the mightiest navy the world has ever known.

To the Brigade of Midshipmen—4,000 strong

—the Naval Academy is more than a home, a campus and a military institution. It is the gangway that leads to the fighting ships of the Fleet. To these future officers the Academy seems almost a part of the sea.

Salt-laden breezes from Chesapeake Bay carry a breath of the sea across three hundred acres of Navy land. Moored at a long sea wall lie "dinghies" and "knockabouts" for small-boat sailing practice. Offshore a fleet of Academy yachts rides at anchor. Over toward the north shore of the Severn 75-foot Yard patrol boats maneuver. Close by, the masts of fishing craft lift above the harbor at Annapolis.

A high, ivy-covered wall separates the historic city of Annapolis and the "yard," as the Academy grounds are called. Anyone who enters the gates looks upon a scene that immediately suggests seafaring.

Roads, walks and lines of trees are laid out with naval precision. Grass plots are kept as clean as a warship's decks. In front of granite buildings stand ancient cannon that flashed, thundered and smoked when wooden sailing frigates fought violent actions. Trophies from America's maritime wars have been enshrined in areas around more than two hundred buildings. Everywhere there are objects which relate to ships and sailors: old-fashioned anchors, links of chain, pyramids of cannon balls and figureheads from famous ships.

Many of the sounds heard at this school for naval officers suggest the sea. The huge 2,500-pound bell in the tower of Mahan Hall strikes ship's time every half hour. Aircraft of the modern Navy roar above relics of the past. Stirring martial music and the rhythmic tread of marching feet announce formations and parades. On Sundays the strong voices of midshipmen carry beyond the chapel; they rise with an inspiring plea at the end of the hymn, "Eternal Father Strong to Save":

Oh, hear us when we cry to Thee
For those in peril on the sea.

The center of life at the Academy is Bancroft Hall. Its rooms and corridors cover fifty acres, thus making it the largest dormitory in the world. It was named in honor of George Bancroft, the Secretary of the Navy who started the school at Annapolis in 1845. From the upper floors of this giant building, rooms of the midshipmen overlook the water. In the cavernous basement are barber shops, stores, kitchens, medical and dental facilities and a post office. Bancroft also contains reception rooms, recreation halls, the soda fountain (called the Steerage), rifle and pistol ranges, and other spaces that make it a city in itself.

The midshipmen's day starts at Bancroft Hall with the six-fifteen clanging of electric gongs. In less than one minute all hands must be out of bed and at attention for a check by the Officer of the Watch. Half an hour later the Brigade is in formation outside. After roll call twenty-four companies march to breakfast in the huge mess hall that adjoins Bancroft.

The simply furnished rooms are ready for a series of inspections before classes commence at eight. Recitations continue until four with an hour break for dinner at noon. Athletics and practice drills in boats or on the rifle range fill in the time until supper at seven. Midshipmen are then free for recreation and extracurricular activities. At eight-fifteen the gongs sound again to mark the start of a two-hour study period. At ten-fifteen the day ends with the sounding of tattoo. In five minutes the lights go out in Bancroft Hall.

The academic grind stops at noon Saturday. Unless restricted, midshipmen may go to Annapolis, attend athletic contests or watch movies. On Sunday they can sleep late, but everyone must attend some church service.

7

The Naval Academy operates under the same strict discipline as ships of the Fleet. Midshipmen give snappy salutes to officers. Orders are acknowledged with a smart, "Aye aye, Sir!" Dress, bearing and conduct follow regulations. This rigid system is the keel on which naval leadership is built.

Compared with a civilian college the Academy is rugged. Military regimentation and specialized training for sea warfare are only parts of a hard curriculum. A midshipman must earn a Bachelor of Science degree in engineering that would require five years at any other good technical institution. In addition his program includes compulsory athletics, the liberal arts and social activities. Summer vacations are spent at sea or for such training as aviation and amphibious war. The casualties among midshipmen are high: one out of five boys who enter does not graduate.

Despite the prospects of hard work, strict supervision and constant discipline, thousands of young Americans try to enter the Naval Academy. They believe that attending the Naval Academy brings honor and prestige. And to most young men graduation represents a tremendous achievement.

The majority of the midshipmen in the Brigade today began thinking of a naval career about the time they entered high school. A few had seen the Academy as Navy Juniors, the children of naval officers. Most knew only what they had heard, read or seen in the movies and on television. From one source or another they learned about the requirements for admission and how to go about obtaining an appointment.

To be eligible for a midshipman's appointment today a boy must be an unmarried U.S. citizen of good character. To pass mental examinations he needs at least a high school education. Physically he must have no defects. He can be no less than five feet, four inches tall and no more than six feet six. He must weigh at least 112 pounds, but no more than 235. In age he has to be between seventeen and twenty-two. No applicant is barred because of race, color or religion.

There are a number of ways for a qualified boy to obtain an appointment to the Academy. The Vice President and members of Congress nominate young men from all the states. The President selects seventy-five applicants by competitive examination from among sons of armed forces officers. Three hundred and twenty applicants are chosen from the regular and reserve forces of the Navy and Marine Corps. A maximum of twenty honor graduates of honor military or naval schools and the Naval Reserve Officers Training Corps are taken each year. Sons of deceased officers and the sons of Medal of Honor holders are entitled to appointments. To fill any gap the Secretary of the Navy makes selections. In all, about 1,200 boys report to the Naval Academy for admission as midshipmen every year.

Successful candidates arrive at Annapolis from every State and Territory. They come from rich, poor and middle-income families. Some have behind them only four years of high school. Others have attended and even graduated from college. Many took regular or postgraduate courses at private prep schools. Each candidate is required to deposit $100 as part payment of the costs of uniforms, textbooks, etc. The balance of $600 due is paid gradually through monthly deductions from his pay as a Midshipman, U.S. Navy.

A typical entering class reports to the Naval Academy in late June. On First Day, suitcases are checked and induction begins with the processing of papers. Almost immediately the new midshipmen, Fourth Class, are in a whirlwind of activity. They are divided into crews of four-teen, each with a coxswain or leader. The crews pass in fast-moving lines to be assigned rooms, laundry numbers, stencils and the first issue of books and clothing. New men rush between the Steerage and their rooms, loaded with gear. Rapid-fire directives order them to get regulation haircuts (no more than three inches on top); begin stenciling all white clothing; see the tailor for the fitting of uniforms.

Midshipmen are warned repeatedly to read the pamphlet, SPECINST (Special Instructions) and understand a large part of it before the end of First Day. This book gives detailed information about the Naval Academy. Naval terms are explained and the locations of various buildings are given.

Perhaps the greatest immediate change from civilian life is the system of time used at the Academy. In SPECINST the baffled new men are advised:

Time is designated in the Navy by four digits, the first two digits indicating the hour counting from midnight, and the second two digits indicating the minutes past the hour.

THUS 0037 IS 37 MINUTES PAST MIDNIGHT

0415 IS 4:15 A.M.

1200 IS NOON

1350 IS 1:50 P.M.

2217 IS 10:17 P.M.

The designations A.M. and P.M. are not used.

After a hectic morning and a quick noon meal, the crews begin getting ready for their final break with civilian life. They assemble for infantry instruction and by late afternoon have been taught enough so they can march to Bancroft Hall. There, in Memorial Hall, groups line up before a flight of marble steps. An officer looks the new men over and says a few words. They are about to be sworn into the United States Navy as midshipmen.

Serious-faced young men listen and look up beyond the officer to a battered blue flag whose uneven white letters read:

DONT GIVE UP
THE SHIP

Those were the dying words of gallant young Captain James Lawrence as he was carried below from the quarter-deck of the frigate *Chesapeake*. The message was hoisted aloft by Commodore Oliver Hazard Perry a short time afterward at the Battle of Lake Erie, one of our many sea victories in the War of 1812. The flag was preserved, and ever since the words have been a motto for American naval officers, in war and peace.

The lads facing the old flag are told to raise their right hands. As the officer administering the oath says these words, they repeat:

I, ..., having been appointed a midshipman in the United States Navy, do solemnly

swear (or affirm) that I will support and
defend the Constitution of the United States
. . . and that I will well and faithfully dis-
charge the duties of the office on which I
am about to enter; So help me God.

The sworn-in candidates are officially midshipmen in the United States Navy and members of the Plebe or freshman class. For the
next few days they are busy learning how to
stow their lockers, how to wear the first of
more than twenty uniforms, and what privileges they have and do not have as Plebes.

To impress on midshipmen the importance
of regulations, the Academy has a system of
giving demerits or marks for bad conduct. If
a midshipman collects more than 300 demerits
in his Plebe year, he may be dropped for un-
satisfactory conduct.

Demerits are given for such things as whis-
tling at girls, having a disorderly room, exhib-

iting poor table manners, having pets in quarters and many other minor offenses. More serious infractions carry demerits plus certain hours of extra duty such as additional drill and standing of watch. The most serious "Class A" offenses—marrying, cheating or owning an automobile—mean dismissal.

From the beginning Plebes learn the importance of standing watch in the Navy, for the man who "has the watch" is responsible for detecting anything that might suggest danger. The penalty for slackness at sea can be the loss of battles, ships and human lives. The demand for alertness on the bridge of a ship is greater than ever today and the Plebe learns this even before he steps aboard.

As he stands watch and learns other routines during the first summer, the Plebe is directly under young officers in the nine departments that guide him through summer indoctrination.

He has no contact with upper class midshipmen until the start of the fall term. The First and Third Classes (seniors and sophomores) are at sea on summer cruises. The Second Class (juniors) have aircraft and amphibious warfare training until they go on their twenty-five day leave.

The officers and civilian instructors whom the new Plebe meets recognize that he is undergoing drastic change. They assure him that by learning to get in step he is not losing his individuality. Rather, he is becoming a member of the Navy's "fighting team" in which he can take great pride.

The small classes of Plebe Summer demand daily recitations as well as written work. No one is permitted to fall behind even in the indoctrination courses. Each summer course—naval history, personal hygiene, marine engineering, gunnery and seamanship—points up the need to build a good foundation and grow step by step.

Since very few incoming midshipmen know anything about seamanship and navigation, courses in that department begin with the simplest things. Men who will one day command atomic-powered vessels first learn to knot and splice line and to row a boat. The same lessons were taught to young men at Phoenician seaports 1,000 years before the birth of Christ.

"Elementary Seamanship" is the title of a pamphlet that introduces Plebes to the ancient arts of handling small boats under oars and sails. The foreword to that text includes a significant paragraph:

> . . . Our weapons and ships continually become more complex; electronics, nucleonics and automation are among the fields in which advancement are rapid. Nevertheless, I guarantee that throughout your naval career, whether you are on the sea, below

the sea, or above the sea, your understanding and knowledge of seamanship will stand you in good stead.

After the Plebes learn to row a whaleboat, they go on to learn how to sail two sizes of sloops—dinghies and knockabouts. They are then ready to handle the yawl-rigged, 44-foot racing yachts. Next they learn to operate motor launches and maneuver the 75-foot YP (Yard Patrol) boats.

After a year of small-boat experience, midshipmen make their first summer cruise in a large naval vessel. Here again they start at the bottom in mastering the ship's operation. During their second cruise, made the summer before graduation, they learn the duties of junior officers.

All other Academy courses follow a similar pattern and are directed toward seamanship—the *sea*, the *man* and the *ship*. With each year of scientific advance in ships, guns and aircraft, studies become more difficult. But almost any young man with average intelligence and with the will and determination to work, can make the grade.

At the start of fall term many a Plebe wonders if he can make the grade. For then the three upper classes are back in full force, and they begin their own informal training of the Plebes. They demand that new midshipmen give correct answers to a wide variety of questions—some serious, many ridiculous.

To survive, the Plebe must memorize all Academy cheers and songs and a number of stock nonsense replies to such questions as, "How's the cow?" and "Why didn't you say sir?" He must be able to state instantly what is on the menu for the next meal or what is being shown at the movies in Annapolis. Keeping a mass of unrelated information in mind ready for recitation is supposed to teach the Plebe to think accurately and quickly under pressure.

With the return of the upperclassmen, the Plebe must start to walk "braced up"—that is, with his chin in and chest out. He "squares" corners in making turns, sits on the front three inches of his chair in the mess hall, and keeps head and eyes facing forward—"in the boat."

The miseries of Plebe year today are mild compared with what Plebes once went through. In the early days, boys were beaten, humiliated and even tortured as a part of hazing.

Today a midshipman's principal worry is keeping up his grades. Each term he faces a new series of exams, or more "rivers to cross." The goal is a perfect score—4.0—but many a midshipman is grateful to get 2.5, the lowest passing grade. When graduation is certain, First Classmen can sing the song "No More Rivers to Cross."

Even in this center of scientific learning, men take steps to assure good luck on exams.

Plebes soon learn that the bronze statue of the famous Indian *Tecumseh* is the Naval Academy's good luck charm. Accordingly, they toss him pennies on the eve of exams and put their faith in the "God of 2.5." *Tecumseh* is the replica of an old sailing ship figurehead and has become one of the best-loved landmarks at the Academy. Before the Army-Navy game the Chief is daubed with orange, yellow and blue war paint as assurance of a Navy victory.

Studies, drills, practical training and compulsory athletics make midshipmen view the leisure of civilians with envy. But they soon learn to make the most of their limited free time.

At the Academy numerous clubs bring together midshipmen with common hobbies: singing, chess, stamp collecting, boating, photography, model building and radio. Anyone with a flare for writing or art can try out for the staffs of Academy publications: *Trident, The Log, The (Log) Splinter, Reef Points* and *The Lucky Bag*. Musicians turn to the concert orchestra, jazz band and the famous drum and bugle corps —the "Hell Cats." Those with a flare for dramatics belong to "The Masqueraders."

Along with everything else midshipmen have their social life—mostly after passing the hurdle of Plebe Year. On Saturday nights there are "hops" (dances) and members of the faculty open their homes to midshipmen. Many a future Ensign has fallen in love with a Yard Engine, as girls who live at the Academy are called.

By any standard, free time and amusements for midshipmen seem scant. But the Academy is not just a school; it is a part of the United States Navy. And any young man who can get in, get through, and get a commission stands out as a man who has what it takes to make a success out of his life.

The generations of youngsters who have graduated from the Academy have slowly shaped it to the present form. How this was accomplished is a story that began almost two hundred years ago, before the Yard existed. In those days future officers received their training at sea in the early fighting ships of an infant Navy.

II

Early Midshipmen

The rank of midshipman was first used in the British Navy about 1600. When the United States commissioned armed vessels of the Continental Navy to fight Great Britain, we borrowed and retained the grade.

A midshipman was so named because his station was in the middle of the ship. At first he was a boy, or alert young sailor, who ran messages fore and aft from "amidships." Later he became an apprentice officer. He was given charge of a group of men, either at the guns or aloft in the fighting tops (platforms part way up the masts). Midshipmen also had the nickname "Reefers" because they were sent out on the yards to reef, or shorten, sail in stormy weather.

The first American midshipmen were boys of about twelve. Family influence secured them appointments to ships. They went to sea to learn by watching and working. Officers taught them some mathematics and navigation. After three years a midshipman could be examined for a lieutenancy.

The Continental Navy disbanded following the Revolutionary War, but even in those days the need for training officers was recognized. John Paul Jones, America's first great sea fighter, urged that every ship in the Fleet have a little Academy, where the officers should be taught the principles of mathematics and mechanics, when off duty. When in port the young officers should be obliged to attend academies.

It was more than half a century before a regular academy came into existence. But training at sea started in 1798 when the modern Navy was founded with the launching of the frigates *United States, Constitution* and *Constellation.* Those fast, heavily armed sailing ships were commissioned to fight the French who were seizing our merchant vessels.

Aboard the *Constellation* our present Navy Regulations were formulated by Captain Thomas Truxtun, who wrote letters that outlined the duties of officers and men. Captain Truxtun, famous as a privateer in the Revolution and a hero in the *Constellation,* gave these orders to each new midshipman:

duced to the gunner's daughter." David Porter escaped by swimming to a Danish ship and resolved to join our new United States Navy so he could always fight back.

In the *Constellation* Porter encountered naval discipline that was only slightly less harsh than aboard British ships. Captain Truxtun hated England, but he used the same threats of flogging or even hanging which were used in the British navy. Food in the ships of those days was poor and scarce; the work of firing heavy cannon and of handling sail was hard. And 250 men were forced to sleep in hammocks along an unventilated, unlit berth deck no larger than one of today's basketball courts. Only the fear of the whip prevented rebellion.

After one cruise young Porter decided to leave the *Constellation*. But Captain Truxtun did not wish to lose such a promising midshipman. Porter was invited to the cabin for dinner, and the skipper listened to the young man's grievances.

"Why you young dog," the bluff captain roared. "If I can help it, you shall never leave the Navy. Swear at you? Why strike me, sir, every time I do that—up you go a round on the ladder of promotion! As for the First Lieutenant blowing you up every day—why, sir, 'tis because he loves you. He would not see you grow into a conceited young coxcomb. Now lay for'ard, and let's have no more whining!"

Then, as now, midshipmen did not contradict a captain. David went forward and very soon justified Captain Truxtun's faith in him. By his quick thinking and bravery he saved the ship from defeat.

The *Constellation* was cruising through the West Indies on February 9, 1799, when she met the celebrated French frigate *Insurgente*. It had been more than twenty years since Captain John Paul Jones in the *Bon Homme*

Richard won his famous victory over the British *Serapis*. Now the new American Navy was again on trial.

Midshipman Porter was in command of the foretop where Marine sharpshooters and a repair crew had been stationed. In the thick of the battle an enemy cannon ball crashed into the foremast just above the top. The huge topsail tugged at the damaged mast, threatening to split it. That would mean the end of the battle, for the *Constellation's* head sails, needed for maneuvering, depended on the topmast.

Porter saw the deck below hidden in smoke; his voice could not carry above the din of gunfire. He acted on his own. Climbing through a barrage of missiles, he cut the slings that held the topsail yard; as it came down the big sail collapsed. The mast of the *Constellation* was saved, and soon afterward the *Insurgente* surrendered.

Personal instruction received from Captain

Truxtun enabled Porter to pass an oral examination for lieutenant. He held that rank in 1801 when he was captured by pirates off Tripoli during our war against the Barbary States.

In the nine months that he and his shipmates were held as prisoners of war, Porter organized a school for midshipmen. He and other officers of the ill-fated American frigate *Philadelphia* taught navigation, mathematics and naval tactics. This informal school in the prison of a North African castle held classes at about the same time that the United States opened a military academy at West Point.

When America went to war a second time against Great Britain, Porter commanded the 32-gun sloop of war *Essex*. This was the War of 1812, fought to protect American rights on the high seas when the British began to seize our sailors and force them into the Royal Navy. In winning the war we proved the superiority and spirit of our sailors with a series of brilliant victories. Along with the frigates *Constitution* and *United States*, the *Essex* under Captain Porter distinguished herself. She was the first ship to engage and defeat an enemy vessel, H.M.S. *Alert*. And in less than two months Porter took ten prizes.

When he went to sea in the *Essex*, Porter took a ten-year-old boy whom he had adopted. This was David Glasgow Farragut, who later became the first admiral in the United States Navy.

David, a very small boy for his age, held the rank of midshipman and was shown no favors by his foster father. He stood watch, went aloft and acted as messenger, powder boy (carrying bags of explosives), and quarter gunner. Despite his size and extreme youth, David was a brave, earnest little fellow. He was well liked by the officers and men.

Many of the midshipmen in the War of 1812 were thoroughly disliked aboard ship. To fill the expanding fleet, the President made 400 appointments but many of the boys had no business going to sea. Given authority and uniforms the little bullies beat and abused seamen without cause. In turn they were mistreated by their officers and received scant instruction. More than ever, training was a matter of self-instruction.

In those war days the Fleet was a rough school. Young Farragut found himself exposed to the shock of combat without pampering. Years later he recalled the scene of battle aboard the *Essex*:

> I shall never forget the horrid impression made upon me at the sight of the first man I had ever seen killed. He was a boatswain's mate, and was fearfully mutilated. It staggered and sickened me at first; but they soon began to fall around me so fast that it all appeared like a dream and produced no ill effect on my nerves.

David fought in all the *Essex* actions until the ship was overpowered by superior forces. During this time he distinguished himself as an able officer and was even given command of a captured ship. When released at the end of the war, he was only thirteen. Too young to be commissioned a lieutenant, David went ashore to school. But under the guidance of Captain Porter he continued with a naval career and eventually rose to the top. Porter's son, born during the war, followed young Farragut and became the Navy's second full admiral.

In postwar years the Navy declined. Congress refused to authorize a naval academy comparable to West Point. America had begun a great westward expansion, and at the time Indian fighters seemed more important than sea fighters.

Ignored by the government, the Navy did what it could to train officers. Schoolmasters were assigned to the big ships that remained in commission. One vessel was designated a cruising school ship. In an attempt to improve morale, a new midshipman's uniform came into being. It featured a full-dress blue coat with white lining, white breeches, a cocked hat ornamented with blue and gold fringed scroll, and eagle-headed swords.

Makeshift schooling at sea proved a failure. Ten years after the War of 1812, eighty-nine of the Navy's smartest midshipmen reported to New York to take examinations for promotion to lieutenant. Fifty of them failed!

Newspapers now held the midshipmen up for ridicule. The future sea commanders were presented as rowdy boys who spent their free time gambling, drinking and engaging in duels with pistols. They frequented such places as the "Jack-Knife Hotel" and the "Sailor's Last Push," which were noted for bad language and fights.

Parents received a shock when their sons came home from long voyages disfigured by scars and missing teeth. Chewing tobacco and proudly displaying tattoo marks, the midshipmen told awesome yarns of naval life. Peacetime duties included fights with desperate slavers, engagements against pirates, and landing parties that battled savages in tropical jungles. Disease, bad food and hard work prevailed in ships of the Fleet.

Naval officers dedicated to the service bombarded Congress and the Secretary of the Navy with appeals for a naval academy. Writers blasted politicians who stood in the way of future naval preparedness. But all that came of this activity was the opening of schools aboard ships docked in New York and Norfolk.

The shore-based school ships and a classroom in a sail loft at Boston were poorly attended. So low was the pay of instructors that only the poorest teachers took the employment. Ambitious midshipmen obtained leaves of absence to attend Yale, Trinity and other colleges. One man even went to West Point.

The coming of the steamship finally made a regular shore school possible. When the Navy ordered two engine-driven warships in 1839, the need for scientific training became apparent. The principles of steam engineering could not be taught aboard a sailing ship. That year the Philadelphia Naval School was established with a one-year course.

Thirty midshipmen from the Fleet reported to the Naval Asylum or old sailors' home, at Philadelphia. They were directed to a wing of the building set aside for their use. These students represented about one-tenth of the midshipmen then in the Navy. Each was required to have served three years at sea.

The Naval School offered few comforts. Rooms with bars on the windows measured eight feet square. Insufficient food prepared by the wife of a retired gunner had a shipboard flavor. No recreation facilities existed.

During study time there were constant interruptions by many of the one hundred old sailors who liked to yarn about the past. When the midshipmen had free time from the concentrated course, they wandered around Philadelphia. Those invited to social functions needed to borrow various articles of clothing to make a complete and presentable appearance.

The rough and reluctant midshipmen managed to remain at the Naval School largely because of the influence exerted by their young mathematics professor, William Chauvenet. He was only twenty years old, but already he had a nation-wide reputation as a scholar. His friendly interest and understanding impressed the sailors.

Fired with the dream of a great naval school, Chauvenet spent his free time getting equipment. He bought second-hand desks and black-

boards. Paper and pens came from the over-
stock of Washington offices. Sextants and
chronometers were borrowed from the Fleet.

When he went to Congressmen with a naval
education plan, Chauvenet was ignored. In the
early 1840s legislators had only one interest in
midshipmen: Naval Academy appointments
were valuable in paying off political favors.
This created a real scandal when it was revealed
that Congressmen had influenced the President
to approve almost half of a year's appointments
to boys in Virginia, Maryland and the District
of Columbia.

A much greater scandal broke in the winter
of 1842. In December the training brig *Somers*
anchored in New York and brought shocking
news. Midshipman Philip Spencer had been
tried for mutiny, found guilty by the captain,
and was hanged at sea. Spencer had a record
for troublemaking, but he was the son of the
Secretary of War.

"Murder or mutiny?" was the question asked by newspapers when the skipper of the *Somers* came to trial. Bitter discussion followed the captain's acquittal. Gradually public opinion supported the plan for a dignified training program to make sure that future naval officers would be of high calibre. Before the feeling died, a new Secretary of the Navy, George Bancroft, acted for the midshipmen.

III

Annapolis

George Bancroft was a well-known historian and teacher when President Polk appointed him to head the Navy in 1845. From his study of America's past, Bancroft knew how vital the Navy could be to national security. He also knew of the many failures to establish a first-class naval academy. The former educator proceeded to outmaneuver Washington politicians.

Even the most active enemies of naval expansion found no fault with Bancroft's request that the Navy be given a deserted Army barracks at Fort Severn on the Severn River. The bleak acreage with decrepit, hundred-year-old buildings adjoined Annapolis, far from the prosperous cities of Washington and Baltimore. Congress made sure no money was appropriated to develop Fort Severn.

Bancroft raised funds to open the new naval school by firing eleven shipboard professors and three teachers of language. This yearly saving of $10,000 went into building repairs and the expense of moving from Philadelphia.

Older naval officers approved Bancroft's shore academy because a sailing vessel could be berthed there. Active seamen favored the project when they heard of the appointment of Commander Franklin Buchanan as Superintendent. He was a well-liked and experienced officer. Finally, the military-minded were satisfied when they learned that the instructors would include a West Point graduate, Professor H. H. Lockwood. The Secretary rounded out the faculty with line officers and retained Professor Chauvenet. Many of the mathematician's ideas went into the new two-year curriculum.

Rules and regulations called for a first year at Annapolis, three years in the Fleet, and a return for one more year of study. After three years at sea, midshipmen of any age could enter. Inexperienced boys had to be at least thirteen years of age. Entrance requirements were simple: reading, writing, addition and some knowledge of geography.

On October 10, 1845, Commander Buchanan assembled the eight members of the faculty and fifty midshipmen. Boys scarcely in their teens lined up with bearded, tobacco-chewing veterans to hear "Old Buck" lay down the school's law. Classes in mathematics, physics, navigation and French would be held six days a week from

8:00 A.M. to 4:30 P.M. There would be four hours of study in quarters every night except Saturday. The Superintendent ended his short speech with this warning:

"Let me say that those of you who fail in conduct or study will be promptly restored to your friends."

Life at the new naval school that winter was hard. The stoves did not provide enough heat to melt snow that whipped through paneless windows and wide cracks. Driving rain off the Severn ruined clothing and books. The food was poor. The new boys suffered from the unaccustomed privation. Even sea-hardened midshipmen growled about the accommodations. There was more truth than humor in their song about sailors at sea:

> *Foolhardy chaps, that lives in towns,*
> *What dangers they are all in!*
> *And now lies shaking in their beds,*

For fear the roof should fall in!
Poor creatures how they envies us,
And wishes, I've a notion,
For our good luck, in such a storm,
To be upon the ocean.

The townspeople of staid old Annapolis did not welcome the coming of the midshipmen. The reputation of the young sailors caused people to get off the narrow, cobbled streets at night and close the shutters of their red brick houses. The early antics of the boys confirmed the fears of the inhabitants.

Inside the Yard the authorities had their hands full. After an outbreak of dueling, Commander Buchanan enforced a new type of discipline. On the advice of Professor Lockwood, he inaugurated infantry drill and placed the former West Pointer in charge.

There was a loud and prolonged protest against "sojer" drill, but it continued. The midshipmen nicknamed Professor Lockwood "The Shore Warrior." To show their resentment of the professor, a group painted white checks around the side of his black horse. The frightened animal, resembling a frigate, was sent galloping through the streets of Annapolis at midnight.

Unaccustomed to handling schoolboy pranks, Commander Buchanan was relieved when war was declared in 1846 to settle a boundary dispute with Mexico. He and forty-seven members of the First Class reported to the Fleet in the spring. The midshipmen were commissioned as Passed Midshipmen.

For the few midshipmen who saw action most of their fighting came in landings and the storming of blockhouses in Mexico and California. The presence of the Navy on the Pacific Coast enabled the United States to take California. As a result Congress looked kindly on requests for appropriations for the naval school. Seven acres were added, and some new buildings were erected.

On July 1, 1850, the school received its present name—The United States Naval Academy. That year, 190 Passed Midshipmen joined the Navy list. A new uniform was authorized, and the course extended to four years. At this time the Academy adopted its present system of grading: a perfect grade was 4.0, and the minimum passing mark 2.5.

Old midshipmen out of the fleet now disappeared from the Naval Academy. Rough sailor pastimes gave way to boyish pranks. The town of Annapolis became more orderly as the fun concentrated on officers and instructors.

If the Officer of the Watch jerked open a door, hoping to discover unauthorized visiting, a bucket of water often emptied on his head. When an instructor was spotted tiptoeing down the hall in sneakers, all rooms received warning by the "door salute"—a slamming of doors as he passed which sounded like guns being fired in salute.

One famous practical joke took place in the early 1850s when Fort Severn was made ready to salute an incoming French warship. Upper-classmen, following orders, removed 136 glass windows to prevent their shattering by con-cussion. But the midshipmen neatly stacked the frames directly under the gun muzzles. Once firing commenced, the salute could not be stopped. Every pane was smashed.

When Commander Louis M. Goldsborough took over as Superintendent in 1853, some of the faculty predicted a change in midshipmen's conduct. The new skipper, a towering man with a rumbling sea voice, had been in ships since his eleventh birthday. But the instructors were disappointed at first. The Commander had a great sense of humor and believed in letting the boys have some fun. The professors with the most complaints received little sympathy.

The Superintendent was inclined to judge these civilians by how useful he thought they might be if ordered aloft at night in heavy weather.

Commander Goldsborough brought with him the best of all cures for mischief: hard work. For the first time in almost three hundred years, sea war was about to undergo a radical change. Steam-powered, propeller-driven naval vessels needed officers with new skills. Midshipmen had less time for pranks when faced with such subjects as electricity, steam engineering, analytic geometry and differential calculus. Advances in gunnery made it necessary to understand the operation and effect of five-ton cannon that threw a 74-pound shell for a distance of one mile in four seconds. Altogether new concepts in naval tactics came when ships no longer depended on wind to maneuver.

Older officers continued to swear by sail. The rebuilt *Constitution* came to the Academy as a station ship. Once clear of the land, the auxiliary steam frigates stopped engines and set sail.

Among other virtues claimed for sailing ships was that of teaching alertness and quick thinking. It was also believed—by veterans of the War of 1812—that midshipmen needed the physical toughening provided by life under sail.

Regular summer training cruises were established to keep midshipmen fit and capable. The men stood watches, went aloft in all weather and learned navigation and seamanship at sea. Old-fashioned sea grub, morning washdown with cold salt water, and sleep in hammocks were part of the voyages abroad.

In those days there were no admirals in the United States Navy. When one of our ships reached a foreign port, the captain was often the nation's only representative overseas. Difficulties arose when our highest ranking officer —a commodore—went ashore to discuss im-

Learn to be a seaman, prepare yourself to be an admiral and to command the American fleet. Learn to rig and unrig, to hand, reef and steer; to navigate a ship scientifically and to perform every duty belonging to the highest and the lowest. . . .

I shall always have pleasure in giving encouragement and instruction to such of you as I see merit it, and such as do not I shall have equal pleasure in getting rid of as speedily as possible.

One of the midshipmen assigned to the *Constellation* was David Porter, seventeen-year-old son of a shipmaster. Although a delicate looking boy, he had already proved himself brave and resourceful at sea. In the West Indies Porter had been seized by a British man-of-war. When he refused to join the King's Navy, the captain ordered him flogged with a cat-o'-nine-tails, a punishment then known as "being intro-

portant matters. Other countries maintained diplomatic priority which allowed commodores to talk only with commodores. Until the Civil War we maintained that it was undemocratic to have higher ranking naval officers in imitation of European monarchies.

The first Academy graduate to become full admiral entered at the age of fourteen in 1854. This was George Dewey of Vermont. His father, a doctor, took George to Annapolis after showing him the sights in New York. At Gate Three little George received a handshake and the advice: "Now, my boy, you are on your own."

On his own George learned to chew tobacco and swear. He also had himself tattooed. In his Plebe year he almost "bilged" (flunked out), and the instructors saw little promise for the lad who later became the hero of the Spanish-American War. Dewey did show persistence and worked himself into a safe quarter of the class that graduated in 1858.

In the next few years, midshipmen had an added incentive to work hard. Trouble over the question of slavery was growing between the states of the North and South. War seemed a certainty.

IV

A Divided Navy

The coming of the Civil War created a terrible crisis for teen-age midshipmen from the South. When states below the Mason-Dixon Line began to secede in January of 1861, these young men were forced to make decisions even mature men found hard. If they left the Academy, it meant breaking a solemn oath to defend the Constitution of the United States. On the other hand, loyalty to the government would make it necessary to renounce their families in the South and perhaps eventually kill some of their boyhood friends.

On the eve of hostilities an atmosphere of gloom hung over the Academy. There were sad farewells as the first Southerners gave up their anchors and buttons and left Annapolis to join the Confederate States Navy. The Southerners who remained did so only after painful inner debate. One of these midshipmen was Robley D. Evans of Virginia, later to be known as Admiral "Fighting Bob" Evans, the most dramatic naval leader of his time.

Evans' younger brother joined the Confederate Army. In his book, *A Sailor's Log,* Evans tells of his own experience:

I concluded to stick by "The Old Flag" and let my family ties look after themselves, and so informed my mother, who was much grieved and shamed by my determination. She finally wrote my resignation, sent it to the Navy Department, where it was accepted, and without previous warning I found myself out of the service. . . .

Authorities were able to have fifteen-year-old Evans reinstated.

Before long family loyalty again involved the boy. After the declaration of war Evans went on a short leave to visit his uncle. One night he decided to eat oysters at a favorite place on the Potomac River. Suddenly, through a gap in the crowd, he recognized his brother in civilian clothes at a far end of the restaurant. The boys pretended not to know each other. Evans struggled with his conscience as the Confederate Army officer in mufti made a hasty exit. He knew just where his brother would hide a skiff after crossing the river. It was his duty to call the provost guard, but that would mean imprisonment and probably death for his own brother.

Evans finished his oysters, ordered another dozen and finally did his duty. By that time his brother had escaped. Dejected, Evans returned to the Academy with a reasonably clear conscience.

Almost immediately after the Civil War opened, Annapolis was in combat territory. Academy gates were locked and under guard because Maryland was expected to secede from the Union. Mobs gathered outside to hurl rocks over the wall and jeer. Midshipmen returned the missiles and the insults.

A rumor spread that the Confederates planned to storm the Academy and seize the *Constitution*. Boat parties of armed midshipmen crossed to the north shore of the Severn to scare off an enemy cavalry company. Midshipmen were deployed to cover the landing at Annapolis of Colonel Benjamin Butler's 8th Massachusetts Volunteers.

Late in April the Navy decided to abandon the Academy. The *Constitution* was made ready for sea and on the twenty-fourth the Battalion lined up to sing "The Star-Spangled Banner" and "Hail Columbia." The midshipmen were dismissed and given ten minutes for farewells. Then the famous old frigate was towed down Chesapeake Bay with 200 midshipmen aboard and proceeded to Newport, Rhode Island. The *Constitution* was followed by the transport *Baltic*, which carried professors, records, books and apparatus. For the duration of the Civil War, the resort city of Newport was the site of the Academy.

In May 112 midshipmen of the three upper classes went to the Fleet as ensigns. This new grade replaced that of Passed Midshipman because in the event of capture its exchange value

equaled seven privates or seven ordinary seamen.

The desperate need for officers brought a
proposal to send even the Plebes to sea immediately. The Commandant of Midshipmen,
Lieutenant Christopher R. P. Rogers, success-
fully protested. But he was turned down when
he suggested that he be given some practice
ships: "in which I might take the midshipmen
to the enemy's coast, and there teach them
their duty afloat in actual war service. . . ."

Ships were too scarce to be allocated to
training. The temporary Academy had to be
content with the *Constitution* and another station ship, the *Santee*. When a new class of 200
boys was inducted, these vessels became quarters. Upperclassmen moved to the once fash-
ionable Atlantic House, a famous hotel whose
columned porch and many windows identified
it with luxury living.

Navy critics raised a howl against the location of the Academy. In a desperate war the vacation spot of America's wealthiest people was called a poor choice for a training site. Protestors claimed that beautiful women, extravagant parties and other temptations would undermine the character of the young men.

Actually Newport was a dull, uncomfortable place for midshipmen. Plebes slept in hammocks slung along crowded berth decks. They turned out at 6:00 A.M. and climbed up the rigging to the masthead and down before eating a breakfast of salt pork, hardtack and weak coffee. Classes, study and seamanship went on all day with breaks only for infantry drill under a broiling sun or on a field swept by wind, snow and sleet.

Recreation at the "gay resort" was almost non-existent. To forestall criticism the authorities declared as out of bounds all theaters, saloons, dance halls and most restaurants. A cake shop found selling pastry flavored with wine went on the black list. Persons extending invitations to midshipmen were assumed to be of questionable character until proved acceptable. The Battalion longed to get away and into action.

To Newport came exciting stories about recent graduates and names well known around the Academy. Professor Lockwood went into the Army and later commanded a brigade at Gettysburg. Commander Buchanan, first Superintendent, joined the Confederate States Navy and commanded the radical new ironclad *Merrimac*, which threatened to destroy the entire Union Navy.

When the Confederate ship *Merrimac* was checked in her second foray, Midshipman Harden Littlepage was aboard. He had been in the first class graduated from Newport before ensigns' commissions were issued. Following the famous battle between the *Merrimac* and the *Monitor*, Littlepage wrote this description of the strange United States vessel:

We thought at first it was a raft on which a boiler was being taken to the shore for repairs, and when suddenly a shot was fired from her turret we imagined an accidental explosion of some kind had taken place on the raft.

After the even battle, the North and South both used the name *monitor* to designate a new type of warship.

Wooden frigates were still in use, but young men going into either navy served in the strange experimental vessels. Some were "rams," which had heavy prows designed to sink the enemy by collision. On the rivers, where much of the naval warfare was fought, both navies used "pook boats" which were light-draft, heavily armed scows.

An innovation of the Civil War was the "David," a propelled mine whose crew guided it at night to the side of an enemy ship where it was made fast. A time fuse was ignited, and the crew swam for safety. Casualties among David crews ran high.

A lucky David commander was William Baker Cushing who was discharged from the Academy in 1860 for bad conduct. He redeemed himself by leading a successful David attack against the ironclad Confederate ship *Albemarle*. Although Cushing escaped death, his body and mind were ruined. Nevertheless, he was awarded the Medal of Honor, promoted to Lieutenant Commander and given $50,000 prize money. Today a headstone in the Naval Academy Cemetery recalls his heroism.

The South had no shipyards and so depended on Davids and on offshore raiders purchased in England. Among those famous corsairs were the *Alabama,* the *Shenandoah* and the *Florida,* which captured and sank millions of dollars' worth of Union shipping.

When Confederate raiders began capturing ships off the New England coast, U.S. Midshipmen spent their summers on cruises of patrol. Additional ships were assigned to the Academy for this duty, and excitement ran high. Although no contact was ever made with the enemy, the expectation boosted morale.

One of the Academy practice vessels was the sloop of war *Macedonian*. As was the custom at the time, she had been named after the British ship defeated in the War of 1812. The *Macedonian* cruised to Europe on lookout for the *Alabama*, which had sunk or seized sixty-four Union ships. Her skipper was Lieutenant Commander Stephen B. Luce, who became famous for his textbook, *Seamanship*, published during the war. Another officer aboard, Alfred Thayer Mahan, later gained renown for his writings, especially *The Influence of Sea Power Upon History*. Officers of this type were charged with getting midshipmen through a wartime cram course.

While the official United States Naval Academy operated at Newport, the South was forced to form a new school. Officers were needed to man the raiders, river boats and harbor defenses. In 1863 the Confederate States Naval Academy opened aboard the gunboat *Patrick Henry*. The ship lay at anchor in the James River just below Richmond, Virginia.

Captain William H. Parker was appointed Superintendent. He had been an honor student in the first class graduated from Annapolis and tried to pattern his new command after the United States Naval Academy. But the sixty midshipmen—boys between fourteen and sixteen years of age—did almost as much fighting as studying.

During the siege of Richmond, Southern midshipmen, armed with cutlasses and carbines, defended Drewrys Bluff. Once fifty of them repulsed the advance troops of a Union force of 30,000 men. Along with combat experience ashore and on the James River, the midshipmen learned to subsist on wartime rations. Because of the blockade, food was scarce. Only two meals a day were served aboard the *Patrick Henry*. For breakfast the men ate hardtack and drank sweet-potato coffee. Dinner consisted of salt pork and corn meal.

Southern midshipmen came from the wealthiest families. Most of them had received a good education before joining the Confederate States Navy. In one of the classes was Raphael Semmes, Jr., son of the famous *Alabama* skipper, who later commanded the James River Squadron.

The Confederate States Naval Academy played a dramatic role ashore after the fall of Richmond in early April, 1865. The small battalion of midshipmen was assigned to load and guard the remains of the Confederate States treasury aboard the last evacuation train. Half a million dollars in silver bricks, gold ingots and

Mexican coin was stowed in boxes. Its destination was the Georgia border, five hundred miles to the south.

With fixed bayonets, the sixty midshipmen of the disbanded Academy fought off looters as the train pulled away one hour before Union troops swarmed into Richmond. For the next month the treasure cavalcade pushed onward over ravished land.

At night midshipmen stood sea watches outside of barns and caves. They fought off bands of half-starved "bummers" and freed slaves. When the train was stopped by ripped-up rails, the money had to be stowed in bags and loaded on horses. When the animals foundered, boxes were used again. Midshipmen loaded them onto man-hauled wagons and abandoned gun carriages.

Day and night all hands kept a sharp lookout for Union scouts who had orders from Washington "to take measures to intercept the rebel chiefs and their plunder, said to be fifteen millions in gold."

Another responsibility was taken on when Mrs. Jefferson Davis, wife of the Confederate president, joined the midshipmen with her small children. It was feared she would be kidnaped and held for ransom. The Davis family was hidden in a battered ambulance.

The half million dollars was delivered safely one month after it left Richmond. Midshipmen were commended and paid off; none of them surrendered or was paroled.

The close of the Civil War meant the end of naval careers for all midshipmen and officers who had served the Confederate cause. Some continued to follow the sea in the American and British merchant marines. Some went to posts abroad. Most of the C.S.N. officers were treated little better than their admiral, Franklin Buchanan.

The former Superintendent of the Naval

Academy was without funds and had been badly injured in action. When he returned to the Eastern Shore of Maryland, twenty-five miles from Annapolis, "Old Buck" found his home burned to the ground. He never again went to sea or to the nearby Academy. But in later years his name was given to the road on which the present Superintendent's house is located.

Another great naval officer who suffered from the bitterness that followed the Civil War was Matthew Fontaine Maury. He was one of those midshipmen who came up the hard way in the sailing frigates of the 1820s and was a champion of the Academy. At the outbreak of the war he held a world-wide reputation as an oceanographer. Because he went with his native state, Virginia, bigoted scientists declared his theories on winds and currents were unsound. Maury ended his life a civilian, but he was elected to the Hall of Fame. Today the Academy honors his name with Maury Hall, which houses the

Department of History, English and Government.

For Northern officers the Civil War brought honor, promotion and the prospect of a bright future. The Fleet had grown to seven hundred ships, officer personnel to seven thousand. The United States Navy was the most powerful, modern and battle-seasoned in the world.

David Glasgow Farragut, who had led Union sea forces, was named the first full admiral in the Navy. Second in rank and destined to succeed him was his foster brother David Dixon Porter. When the midshipmen returned to Annapolis from Newport, Admiral Porter was named Superintendent of the Academy. More of the past was recalled in September, 1865, as the old frigate *Constitution* sailed up Chesapeake Bay with the Battalion of Midshipmen aboard. During the passage south, the remarkable "Old Ironsides" crowded on canvas to log

13½ knots. That speed bettered the average of the steamship *Persia*, holder of the transatlantic record. Naval men saw a good omen in the performance.

Good fortune would be needed at Annapolis to keep the Academy afloat.

V

The Perils of Peace

Midshipmen who landed from the *Constitution* viewed a desolate scene within the walls of the Yard. Faculty members could barely believe their eyes. The Naval Academy had never been elaborate, but neither had it been allowed to reach the state in which the Army left it at the end of the Civil War.

Horses had trampled shrubs and chewed

leaves off the young trees. Ramshackle huts that had been soldiers' beer halls spotted the parade grounds. Papers, broken glass and discarded clothing littered the Yard. The Superintendent's house showed the scars of having served as a billiard hall and saloon. Midshipmen's dormitories, used as hospital wards, smelled of disinfectant and death.

Admiral Porter viewed the wreckage with a seaman's eye. All hands were turned to, getting the grounds and buildings shipshape. The veteran of three wars, who had been mentioned prominently as a successor to Abraham Lincoln as President of the United States, was not likely to be taken aback by slovenliness.

Admiral Porter was a big handsome man and, even at fifty years of age, an athlete. To some he presented a formidable appearance with his deep voice and square-rigged, foot-long beard. But he was a hero to midshipmen who sensed his interest in their welfare. He was a man of

73

action whose career had been filled with adventure.

David Dixon Porter had gone to sea at the age of ten when his father took service with the Mexican Navy. He fought hand-to-hand battles with Spaniards in the Caribbean and was captured. After being released from a Cuban prison, he joined the United States Navy as a midshipman.

Like his famous father, Porter first served in the *Constellation*. He commanded a ship in the Mexican War and with the coming of peace secured inactive status so he could sail in the merchant marine. Among his commands was the *Supply*, in which he transported the first camels shipped from the Mediterranean to America. The Civil War saw him rise rapidly in river fighting and harbor sieges.

With the Yard cleaned up, Admiral Porter received authorization to purchase eighty additional acres and erect new buildings. The most urgently needed structure was a dormitory, for there were now five hundred midshipmen in training. Ground was broken immediately for New Quarters, an ugly, five-story red brick edifice that was replaced by Bancroft Hall forty years later.

The years of Admiral Porter's superintendency are looked back upon as "The Golden Age of the Naval Academy." A new spirit came in those postwar years to make everyone forget the dreary life at Newport and the dull existence at the old Academy.

Ancient subjects and outmoded regulations were discarded. The Battalion was reorganized into four divisions of six gun crews each. Pay was increased to $800 a year, and a new uniform was designed. Even infantry drill became fairly popular when the band received orders to get rid of dingy uniforms and appoint a drum major.

Admiral Porter brought his wife and five of

his children to live at the Yard. His sixth youngster, Theodoric, entered as a midshipman. Other
officers and instructors were encouraged to have
their families live at the Academy and enter a
new social life.

Weekly dances and big celebrations on holi-
days had their beginnings, and the Class of '67
started the custom of identifying classes by
graduation year. The forerunner of today's
yearbook, *The Lucky Bag,* made its appearance. This was *Shakings,* a collection of hu-
morous recollections, named after the shipboard
term that describes odds and ends of waste
rope and snips of canvas.

In 1866 the renowned *Tecumseh* arrived at
the Yard. This former figurehead of the ship
Delaware was originally named after the Indian Chief Tamanend. No one is sure just how
the present name of Tecumseh caught on. A
number of other nicknames were used for short
periods including "Old Sebree," after one of the

midshipmen. Even if the origin of *Tecumseh's* name is vague, the Chief has always represented good luck.

Under Admiral Porter the Academy was administered by the Navy Department. The training course was then fixed at four years of shore training followed by two years at sea. With this stability came the touches that built custom and tradition: class badges, colors and rings; the arrival of Farragut's famous steam frigate *Hartford* as station ship; the start of an honor system that did away with personal prying.

Competitive sports made their appearance at Annapolis, for the Superintendent was a fine boxer and all-round athlete. Regularly he put on boxing gloves and sparred with the heavier midshipmen. He ordered the guns of Fort Severn removed to make way for a gymnasium. He also encouraged sailing races and led the way to forming class baseball teams.

In the Academy fleet was the famous racing

yacht *America*. This swift 171-ton schooner had beaten traditionally superior British craft in 1851 to win the Royal Yacht Squadron Queen's Cup. The *America,* sold many times, had been a blockade runner in the Civil War. After her capture she was turned over to the Academy and Admiral Porter had her overhauled. This led to false charges of extravagance.

Critics of naval spending used the *America* to focus unfavorable publicity on Annapolis. Newspapers received reports about "Porter's Dancing Academy" with emphasis on the gay life led by midshipmen at a time when the nation suffered from depression and strife.

Elderly officers, still active in their fight to preserve the ways of 1812, came down to Annapolis to inspect the newfangled Academy. They looked with scorn at the many cutaway models in the engineering building. They blew up at the practice of holding dances. The presence of theatricals and pretty young women shocked the old seamen.

Congressmen who had been thwarted when they sought to get Academy entrance requirements eased lent sympathetic ears to the complaints of the critics. But the Academy had been given a strong new start which helped withstand even greater perils than criticism. Admiral Porter completed his tour of duty as Superintendent in 1869 and would always be remembered as the father of the modern U.S.N.A.

In 1870 bad times came to Annapolis in the wake of Fleet troubles. Warships built of green timber began to fall apart. Many vessels foundered at sea; others were laid up. Then personnel felt the hump that always follows a war: young men had been upgraded so rapidly that promotion from the lower ranks was slow now. The Academy felt the pinch when Congress enacted a law that deprived midshipmen of their rank. They were graded as "cadet midshipmen."

Through the next ten years the Navy continued to lose strength. From a fleet of more than seven hundred warships it slipped to a total of thirty-one. And only four of those vessels were iron steamers. With so few billets and with the officers' list at 2,000, Academy graduates faced a long wait for promotion. Congress acted unfavorably again in 1882 by classifying students at Annapolis as "naval cadets." Graduates were honorably discharged if no vacancies existed at sea. The magazine, *Harper's Weekly,* called the Navy "an asylum for old age and a grave for youthful ambition."

With low morale came the first appearance of hazing—the mistreatment of Plebes by upperclassmen. Previously, the Academy had looked with scorn on this practice of beating and bullying new boys; it was an activity engaged in only by West Pointers and college undergraduates.

There were hundreds of hazing devices that included paddlings, dips in the winter waters of the Severn, torturing acts and such cruel, frightening rituals as branding or cutting a blindfolded Plebe with a piece of ice.

As soon as the mishandled Plebes became Youngsters, they took their turn punishing the incoming class. Investigations, demerits, loss of privileges and dismissal did not cure hazing. The practice led to even more destructive acts. Cadet Philo Norton McGiffin was severely punished for a prank that showed the rebellious spirit brought on by bad times. He rolled cannon balls down the stairs of New Quarters. The heavy round shot tore away bannisters and crushed walls before plummeting through the ground floor. McGiffin later joined the Chinese Navy.

The troubles of the 1870s and 1880s were a

severe test of the motto DON'T GIVE UP THE SHIP. More than a few officers and cadets carried on.

Albert A. Michelson, Class of '73, returned to the Academy as an instructor five years after graduating. With ten dollars' worth of mirrors and other simple equipment he found in the Naval Academy laboratories, he made the first device to measure the speed of light. This experiment between the sea wall and one of the Yard buildings became the basis of future astronomical research. Michelson resigned from the Navy and went on to become recognized as one of the world's foremost physicists.

One of Michelson's classmates, Bradley A. Fiske, remained in the Navy and invented the torpedo plane, the telescopic sight, and an electromagnetic system for exploding torpedoes. These and other inventions helped Fiske rise in prominence. He was later promoted to the rank of rear admiral.

Official U.S. Navy Photograph

Above: This is the Main Gate to the Naval Academy. Guards check every car entering the Academy, which is separated from the town of Annapolis by a high wall.

Below: Midshipmen march in military formation into Bancroft Hall, the Naval Academy dormitory which houses over 2,000 men.

Acme Photo

This side view of the Naval Academy Chapel is seen from the Superintendent's quarters. The Chapel seats 2,000 midshipmen.

Above: The official seal of the United States Naval Academy.

Below: The crypt of John Paul Jones is located in the Chapel of the Naval Academy.

The large building in the foreground is the new Field House of the United States Naval Academy. It can seat 12,000 people at graduation. The domed building in the upper left is the Chapel. The great sprawling building in the upper right is Bancroft Hall, midshipman dormitory.

Above: In the early days, midshipmen classes in seamanship studied the complicated rigging of a man of war.

Below: Present-day midshipmen are instructed in the working of boilers and engines as well as navigation by radar.

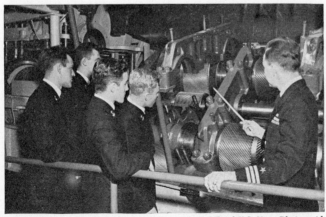

Above: Hard studying, in class and out, is required to pass the very stiff courses at the Naval Academy. When the last exam is passed, midshipmen sing, "No more rivers to cross."

Below: These uniforms are worn by midshipmen on various occasions. "White works," on the extreme left, are for hard labor. The uniform with short jacket and high collar is for dress parade.

Acme

Above: All midshipmen have sailing lessons that begin with these 18-foot sloops called knockabouts.

Below: Even in this age of atomic energy, midshipmen are taught to handle small boats and become expert oarsmen.

Brown Brothers

Official U.S. Navy Photograph

Above: At every Navy football game, Bill, the Academy mascot, parades along the sidelines with his two keepers.

Below: The Brigade of midshipmen stands at attention during dress parade on Worden Field at the Naval Academy. Dress parade is held weekly during the spring and fall.

Official U.S. Navy Photograph

Before an Army-Navy game, midshipmen decorate the statue of Tecumseh with war paint. Presumably this great Indian figure brings good luck to the Navy team.

Above: First and Third Classmen go aboard the USS *Missouri* for an eight-week summer cruise and practical lessons in navigation and seamanship.

Below: Aboard the USS *Leyte* midshipmen on a training cruise shoot flight operations with a Navy camera.

Official U.S. Navy Photograph

Above: Admiral William F. Halsey, on the left, was one of the first officers in the United States Navy to realize the full effectiveness of naval aircraft.

Below: During aviation summer, midshipmen observe takeoffs and landings of naval aircraft. Here a Navy Cougar is being launched from the USS *Oriskany*.

Official U.S. Navy Photograph

Above: A crack company of midshipmen passes in review in the dress parade that precedes Presentation of Colors.

Below: One of the big events of June Week is Presentation of Colors to the company which has earned the honor of carrying Brigade flags for the coming year. Flags are presented by the Color Girl, who is selected by the company captain.

In the 1880s the Navy had started to develop its own scientists and looked to the Academy for men interested in the experiments of the time—such innovations as the Holland submarine and the proposed aircraft of Samuel Langley. Man still had not conquered the air and underseas, but electric lights, phonographs, telephones and the internal combustion engine were in use. Boys were reading the novels of the French author, Jules Verne: *From the Earth to the Moon, Twenty Thousand Leagues Under the Sea,* and *Around the World in Eighty Days.*

The Navy needed highly trained men with great vision. This meant everything possible should be done to attract outstanding boys to the Naval Academy. Age limits for entering midshipmen were raised one year. Now a candidate had to be at least fifteen, no more than twenty. Annual pay of a midshipman was raised to $950.

At the same time young officers were urged

to stay with the Navy. By the end of the nineteenth century the nation was again turning its attention to the Navy. Already Germany was showing power on the high seas. Trouble threatened with Spain over the Administration of Cuba and the Philippine Islands. Only a strong fleet could handle these problems.

A quickly built Navy of 100 new ships put the United States ahead of such maritime nations as Chile and China. The battleship *Indiana* and her three sisters were the fastest and most powerful men-of-war afloat in the 1890s. Each displaced 10,000 tons, steamed at 17 knots and mounted 30 guns, including giant 13-inch cannons. Sides of nickel steel measured a foot and a half in thickness. The fast-firing guns threw 80,000 pounds of metal in thirty minutes. Two seconds after being fired an 850-pound shell could hit an enemy ship one mile off.

Our reborn Fleet, painted white for tropical service, was ready for action when the armored cruiser *Maine* was sunk in Havana Harbor on February 15, 1898. Two hundred and sixty-six American officers and men were killed. In less than two months we were at war with Spain.

On May first Admiral Dewey led seven ships into Manila Bay and destroyed Spain's Asiatic Squadron. Again naval cadets were graduated ahead of time and sent to join vessels in the Caribbean. Hiding in those waters were the remaining ships of Spain's Navy under Admiral Miguel Cervera.

During the summer of the war, forty under-classmen were granted permission to join com-batant ships. Among these naval cadets was a tall slender boy from Ohio. This was Ernest J. King, Class of '01, who saw his first action aboard the protected cruiser *San Francisco*. King graduated fourth in his class and went on to become our Fleet Admiral in World War II.

Another naval cadet who came under enemy fire was F.T. "Kid" Evans. He joined his father.

Captain "Fighting Bob" Evans aboard the battleship *Iowa* just as Admiral Cervera decided to come out of Santiago, Cuba, and fight.

The *Iowa* led the American squadron into brief but fierce action and hoisted the signal that announced victory. Captain Evans received the defeated Admiral Cervera aboard his ship.

The Spanish Admiral and his staff were interned at the Naval Academy until midsummer when an armistice was signed. We had fought a one-sided war, but combat revealed weaknesses in our ships and gunnery. Also, by acquiring new territory in the Pacific and Caribbean, America faced the necessity of building and maintaining a first-rate Navy.

In 1901 Theodore Roosevelt, a navy-minded man, became President of the United States. He was determined that we would not repeat the mistake of allowing our Navy to deteriorate after war.

To show the world that we intended to remain a sea power, Roosevelt ordered Rear Admiral "Fighting Bob" Evans to take the "White Squadron" of sixteen battleships on a 46,000-mile cruise around the globe.

When TR addressed the graduating class of 1902 at Annapolis, he stressed that American officers must have the sea habit to continue our tradition of naval leadership:

> ". . . The best ships and guns and the most costly mechanism are utterly valueless if the men are not trained to use them to the utmost advantage. From now on throughout your lives there can be no slackness. . . ."

VI

"Anchors Aweigh"

The opening years of the twentieth century brought a new look to the Naval Academy. The dynamic Teddy Roosevelt continued to fire the interest of the people in their first line of defense. Boys from every state were eager to become officers in the powerful 200-ship Fleet, and national attention centered on Annapolis. Larger and more modern facilities were needed for the midshipmen, as they again became known. The Battalion had expanded from four to eight companies and on October 26, 1903, made its first appearance as a Regiment.

Orders came to tear down old structures and replace them with the modern granite buildings of today. By the time the White Squadron returned in 1909, ten million dollars' worth of new architecture had risen on the shore of the Severn.

Bancroft Hall, the chapel, the Superintendent's House and halls named after Maury, Mahan and other naval figures brought thousands of citizens to Annapolis to view the world's foremost naval school.

As though to mark the passing of an era, historic Fort Severn was demolished. A few years later the *Santee* sank at her berth. Then Farragut's Civil War flagship *Hartford* departed. It was replaced as station ship by the captured Spanish cruiser *Reina Mercedes*. Another trophy of the most recent war—the foremast of the *Maine*—was set up in the Yard. Since the other mast was preserved at Arlington Cemetery, thirty miles away, midshipmen called the *Maine* "the longest ship in the Navy."

On January 26, 1913, the Academy received an addition as significant as any monument, new or old. On that date the remains of the Navy's first hero, John Paul Jones, were placed in a crypt below the chapel. The great sea commander of the Revolutionary War died in Paris. It took years to locate his unmarked grave, for Jones had passed away in obscurity and near poverty during the time we allowed the Continental Navy to vanish.

National interest was aroused by the return of the first naval officer to suggest an Academy for midshipmen. Nathalia Crane composed a poem urging that Jones' famous ship *Bon Homme Richard* be salvaged from the depths off the southeastern coast of England. But long before, the remains of the broken vessel had been scattered in thirty fathoms.

After almost seventy years the Naval Academy had become a solid part of American tradition. Never again would there be any question about its value so tersely stated on its seal: *Ex scientia tridens,* meaning "from knowledge, sea power." Graduates no longer went to sea on probation. Instead they immediately received commissions as ensigns. With war clouds gathering in Europe there was promise of action and fast promotion again.

While the Academy was undergoing modernization, the Regiment had established the tradition which is most widely known to civilian America—football rivalry with the United States Military Academy at West Point.

The year 1906 saw the twelfth playing of the

famous annual Army-Navy game. That year the midshipmen effectively employed the Rockne innovation, the forward pass, to win by a score of 10-0. This game marked the start of modern American football.

The crowd attending that football game also heard for the first time the stirring Academy march "Anchors Aweigh." The words of the song were written especially for the football classic by Midshipman Alfred Hart Miles. Almost every radio or television listener today recognizes the opening stanza:

> *Stand Navy down the field,*
> *Sails set to the sky!*
> *We'll never change our course,*
> *So Army, you steer shy-y-y-y!*
> *Roll up the score, Navy,*
> *Anchors aweigh!*
> *Sail Navy down the field*
> *And sink the Army; sink the Army gray!*

The fame of the song spread all over the world. When the Army Chief of Staff visited Brazil in 1940, he was embarrassed to be serenaded with "Anchors Aweigh." Native military bands thought it was the national anthem of the United States.

Like "Anchors Aweigh," the Navy football team became the trademark of the Academy. Fans who had never been to college became loyal supporters; they learned the songs, cheers and yells of the midshipmen. Eventually people traveled great distances every year to attend the Army-Navy game at Philadelphia. Between halves, midshipmen and cadets march, bands play and cheer leaders perform. For some fans the half-time show is as important as the game.

A familiar sight at the annual classic is the meeting of the two service mascots: the Army mule and Bill, the Navy goat. To the refrain of "The Battle Hymn of the Republic" midshipmen sing a song about Bill:

The goat is old and gnarly
And he's never been to school,
But he can take the bacon
From the worn-out Army mule.
He's had no education
But he's brimmin' full o' fight,
And Bill will feed
On Army mule tonight!

The first Navy goat appeared in 1890 when the Navy went to West Point to play football for the first time. On the way to the field midshipmen borrowed a goat from a sergeant as a joke. When Navy won, 20-0, the goat was purchased and named Galena Bill, after a famous mascot aboard the *Galena* in the Civil War. The original goat had led a landing party along a path up the steep cliffs of Magnolia

Bluffs, Florida. The sailors hesitated at the sum-
mit. Then the goat butted one of them over,
and his shipmates followed to win the day.

Through the years there have been many goat
mascots, all named Bill. By this time Bill is a
fixed part of Academy football.

In addition to *the* game of the year, the midshipmen play as tough a schedule as any college in the country. And the members of the
team are given no concessions such as snap
courses. They must do the same work as their
classmates. This is possible because no midshipman survives at the Academy with an academic
problem or a hesitancy to work hard.

The heavy scholastic requirements of the
present grew out of the advances about to be
made with the start of World War I. New types
of ships, radio, gyrocompass, oil-burning engines and optical fire control were just a few

of the expanding fields in which a midshipman was expected to master fundamentals before graduation.

The Class of 1916 was the last one to graduate on schedule before the United States went to war against Germany and Austria. The 177 men who were about to receive commissions listened to an address that stressed the future in a way that could apply today. The speaker was Secretary of the Navy Josephus Daniels who told the midshipmen:

> . . . The old things are passing away; new things must be devised. With what weapons, by what strategy shall we meet the terror of the submarine and the still unrevealed possibilities of the airship?

> . . . Who shall say that before you become captains, naval warfare will not undergo a revolution as great as the one that

followed the construction of the *Monitor* and the *Merrimac?*

After the United States declared war on April 6, 1917, Academy graduates in the Fleet experienced the start of the terrible changes predicted by the Secretary. German U-boats (from *Unterseeboot*) sank almost fifteen million tons of Allied shipping. Zeppelins (rigid dirigible balloons) introduced air bombardment when they made night attacks on London. The first fighter planes appeared over France.

Most of the newly commissioned officers who were graduated ahead of time went into Navy-operated troopships or cruisers and other escort craft. Two million American troops were hauled to Europe by the Navy without loss of a single life. Other Annapolis men served in patrol boats, mine layers and armed yachts. Many served at the forty-five air stations in France, and some earned golden wings for flying in war missions.

The Navy fought no fleet actions in the first World War, and most of the glory went to land troops. But the Marine Corps again distinguished itself. The Marines were, as they still are, under the Navy Department with ten percent of each Academy class receiving commissions as Second Lieutenants in the Marine Corps.

Before the Armistice was signed on November 11, 1918, it had become apparent that in future wars the Navy would need to depend on civilian reserves. At the end of the conflict the Fleet numbered 2,000 vessels with 45,000 officers. Most of these men had been recruited and indoctrinated hastily. Except for merchant marine and enlisted personnel, few had any sea experience.

Since the percentage of professional, Academy-trained officers would always be small during a war, the Navy took steps to insure that the regular officers rated high in leadership.

The hard core of Annapolis men would occupy key positions and set an example for reserves.

During World War I the present system of appointing midshipmen was approved by Congress with provisions that included taking men from the enlisted ranks for the Academy every year. In the Fleet efforts were made to advance officers solely on merit rather than seniority.

The greatest concentration was placed on developing leadership in midshipmen. After a postwar outbreak of hazing that led to a Congressional investigation, Rear Admiral Henry B. Wilson took over as Superintendent in 1921. The former Commander of U.S. Naval Forces in France reviewed the hazing problem and set about to solve it with radical action. There was much criticism of the Wilson method, but none of it came from the midshipmen who were soon devoted to "Uncle Henry."

Admiral Wilson dealt directly with classes and their officers. He gained the midshipmen's confidence by listening to their opinions. He decided that the chief motive for hazing was no more than a desire to put Plebes in their place. To accomplish this without bullying, certain privileges and prohibitions were incorporated in Academy Regulations.

Upperclassmen were now permitted to smoke in designated areas. They could travel to Washington and Baltimore and had Christmas leave. The uniform of all midshipmen was modernized to do away with the old-fashioned high collar.

Regulations defined Plebe restrictions. They could not enter Smoke Park, sit on certain reserved benches, or walk in Lovers' Lane. In the future they must proceed to all drill formations "on the double" (running) and memorize all notices posted on the bulletin board in Bancroft Hall. Questions asked by superiors were to be answered promptly and correctly.

The enforcement of the new regulations gave Upperclassmen a substitute for hazing and emphasized the lowly position of the Plebe. He was referred to as "Joe Gish" or "W.T. (watertight) Door," the names of mythical knownothing Fourth Classmen.

During the administration of Admiral Wilson, the Academy concept of honor matured when midshipmen found themselves being treated like men instead of boys. The Naval Academy did not use a formalized honor system. A midshipman was never asked, "Did you break such and such regulation?" What he would hear was, "I am putting you on report." He could then make a statement. The overall feeling is that serious infractions will not occur if midshipmen develop personal integrity.

Everything about the Academy in the first quarter of the twentieth century pointed to progress. The streamlining of buildings, courses and the treatment of midshipmen matched the dramatic change then under way in aviation.

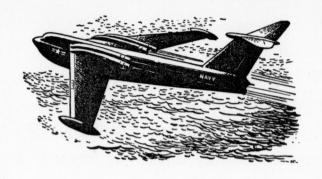

VII

Wings of Steel

Immediately after World War I Congress appropriated fifteen million dollars for a Fleet air arm. Then Naval aviation really took off. Young line officers and new Academy graduates swamped the Navy's flight training base at Pensacola, Florida, with applications. By 1925 it was clear that aircraft would cause another revolution in sea warfare. In June the Naval

Academy inaugurated Aviation Summer for Second Classmen.

The first permanent aviation detail was assigned to the station ship *Reina Mercedes* under two lieutenants who were graduates of Pensacola, called the Annapolis of the Air. Their assignment was to orient each Youngster Class in the theory of flying and take the midshipmen aloft for indoctrination. The basic idea was, and still is, to show midshipmen the part played by aircraft in the Fleet. Those with a yen for aviation could put in for regular pilot's training after graduation.

No one at Annapolis was more impressed by the possibilities of the naval air arm than Captain William F. Halsey. He came to the Yard for duty as skipper of the *Reina Mercedes* early in 1926 and showed an immediate interest in flying. At that time Bill Halsey was forty-three years old—a distinctive figure with large head, heavy jaws and thick eyebrows that emphasized his scowl or grin. He had been up for only two short flights years before, but the idea of using planes intrigued Halsey. One day he would direct them in battles against the Japanese during the Pacific action of World War II.

As skipper of the station ship, Halsey had the two lieutenants billeted there take him aloft. In his great book, *Admiral Halsey's Story*, he recalled:

> It wasn't long before they were letting me handle the controls, and it wasn't much longer before I thought I was an ace. When I said, awhile back, that the arrival of the aviation detachment changed my whole naval career, I was not exaggerating. Soon I was eating, drinking, and breathing aviation, and I continued to do so during the remainder of my duty on the *Reina*.*

* From *Admiral Halsey's Story* by William Frederick Halsey and Joseph Bryan. 1947. McGraw-Hill Book Company, Inc.

Bill Halsey was destined to join John Paul Jones, David Porter and David Farragut as one of the most colorful figures in American naval history. He belonged to that part of the air age which in less than fifty years progressed from engined kites to jets.

The son of a naval officer, Bill was sworn in to the Academy in 1900. Only a fair student, he graduated forty-third in a class of sixty-two. But he was a good football player and held down the fullback position during his last two years. In 1903 Bill and other midshipmen read about the Wright brothers' first successful flight in a power-driven airplane.

Among the lowerclassmen at the Academy with Halsey were some of the pioneers of naval aviation: P. N. L. Bellinger, T. G. Ellyson and John Towers. These men went directly into naval aviation after graduation and were the ones who gave Halsey his first rides.

Those observation hops were taken in 1913. The year before, "Spuds" Ellyson made a successful catapult take-off from a barge. Thirty years later Navy dive bombers and fighters were taking off from the decks of huge carriers.

In 1919 Towers commanded a group of three Navy-Curtis flying boats, in what was then considered a daring operation—a 4,500-mile series of hops across the Atlantic.

These early sea planes were small and slow when compared with the present Navy Martin XP6M-1 Seamaster:

Flying Boat NC-4		*Seamaster (Vcc-)*	
Gross weight	28,000 pounds	600,000	pounds
Speed	110 knots	600	knots
Length	45 feet	200	feet
Wing span	126 feet	200	feet
Crew	6 men	20	men

So fast were changes in aviation that the NCs, or Nancys, had become obsolete long before

Halsey went to the Academy in 1926 and re-
newed his interest in flying. Richard E. Byrd,
Class of 1912, flew over the North Pole in May,
1926. Soon he was preparing to make his 1929
dash across the South Pole. Academy graduates
were helping to develop new kinds of planes,
lighter-than-air craft and systems of aerial navigation. Into commission came the world's first
aircraft carrier, the *Langley,* which was nicknamed "The Covered Wagon."

Even though the Navy led the way with
racing teams and spectacular flights to Rio de
Janeiro, Hawaii and the polar regions, research
and solid invention were the real goals. This
was true even at a time when young people
were lured to aviation chiefly by spectacular
feats and death-defying acts.

Former wartime pilots traveled around the
country putting on air circus performances.
Flimsy planes, held together by baling wire,
flew upside down, did loop-the-loops and hedge-

hopped through the country. Daredevils made low parachute jumps; acrobats balanced on wings and swung from trapezes. Scores of casualties gave a black eye to serious flying.

When Halsey returned to duty with the Fleet, he maintained a strong interest in all phases of aviation. Before taking command of a new carrier he insisted on going through the difficult flight course at Pensacola. He had to extend himself to keep up with young men, but at the age of fifty-one Bill Halsey earned his wings. First-hand knowledge of what was felt by dive-bomber and fighter pilots helped him achieve the great three-day naval and air victory over the Japanese off the Solomon Islands in November, 1942.

The climax of the flying Admiral's career came in Tokyo Bay when the Japanese signed their formal surrender on the deck of the U.S.S. *Missouri*. At the ceremonies with Halsey stood some of naval aviation's pioneers: Admirals

Bellinger, Byrd and Towers. Missing was Spuds
Ellyson, who had died in an early air crash.
Also present was the famous Admiral Marc A.
Mitscher, leader of the fast carrier Task Force
58, the "terror of the Pacific."

Pete Mitscher had entered the Naval Academy from Oklahoma City in 1904. Less than two
years later he was requested to vacate the prem-
ises. A member of Pete's class had been killed
in a fight that grew out of hazing. Two hundred
midshipmen were involved in a Congressional
investigation, and Mitscher—with many demerits and a poor scholastic record—was discharged.

In June of 1906 Pete Mitscher was able to
report back to Annapolis, but he entered the
Academy again as a Plebe. Even with his previous experience he remained a "wooden" student and in 1910 graduated near the bottom
of the class.

Mitscher, a small, even-tempered boy, was a
constant source of surprise to Academy author-

ities. While he did poorly in some subjects, he excelled in others, such as naval warfare. And no one expected so respectful and obedient a young man to get a tattoo that showed a bluish-colored buzzard dripping blood from the wound made by a purple dagger.

Pete Mitscher was one of the individualists who were first attracted to naval aviation and grew up with it in the face of "old school" opposition. When aircraft first became a part of the Fleet, die-hards fought the idea just as strenuously as another generation had battled against steamships replacing sailing vessels.

Soon after graduation Pete reported to Pensacola where he qualified as a pilot in the open seaplanes made of wire, wood and canvas and powered by 100-horsepower pusher engines. He flew one of the Nancys in the 1919 transatlantic operation and went on to specialize in naval and air warfare.

Early in World War II Mitscher commanded

the aircraft carrier *Hornet.* It was from her flight deck that Army bombers took off for a surprise raid over the Japanese home islands. Mitscher had three big carriers shot out from under him in a period of five days by Japanese suicide planes, called *kamikazes.*

The gentle Mitscher remained independent throughout his career. He wore brown shoes instead of regulation black, a fad adopted by navy flyers. And he did not consult regulations when his pilots were in danger.

For years the Navy would talk about the hard decision made by Admiral Mitscher when the delayed planes from his carrier approached for a return after dark, all of them dangerously low on fuel. To turn on lights might mean losing the big ship to a lurking Japanese submarine, but without lights the carrier would be invisible and pilots must crash in the sea. Pete Mitscher gave the light-up order.

The experiences of Navy pilots in World War II and the Korean War have been incorporated in the training program of Aviation Summer. One of the most practical and appropriate phases of instruction is given with the "Dilbert Dunker." The contraption is built like the cockpit of a plane and mounted on skids above the outdoor swimming pool. In this the midshipman crashes into the water and learns how to get himself clear of the wreckage.

Second Classmen learn the duties of flight and air crews and the operation of seaplanes, multi-engined amphibians and helicopters. As observers they go aloft in all types of aircraft including jets; they visit the Glenn L. Martin Aircraft Factory at Baltimore. The final phase of Aviation Summer is a three-week cruise aboard a first-line aircraft carrier. Midshipmen stand the watches of both officers and enlisted men and learn the procedure of carrier plane take-offs and landings.

In thirty years aviation indoctrination has made remarkable changes. At one time midshipmen studied about giant dirigibles, those rigid balloons. These were capable of long and (then) fast flights and could operate at altitudes that made them safe from any plane or anti-aircraft shell.

Today midshipmen study the theory of guided intercontinental missiles, robot planes and the launching of earth satellites. Looming in the not-so-distant future is navigation in the great sea of space where science fiction predicts there will be battles of great complexity.

Current naval aviation is complex enough to keep a midshipman busy just staying abreast of the times. But he is not expected to become an expert in four years. His task is to understand the strength and use of forces that continually change naval warfare. He must know the machines, but also he must know the operating technicians and how to command those men.

VIII

Navy Blue and Gold

About the same time that aviation training was introduced, today's athletic program at the Academy began to expand. It was launched on the wave of sports enthusiasm which swept the United States in the 1920s.

At that time the idols of teen-agers were Babe Ruth, Jack Dempsey, Johnny Weismuller, Bobby Jones and other great athletes. Big crowds attended games, fights and meets; millions tuned in to the new radio broadcasts. Intercollegiate rivalry reached new heights.

In 1926 Navy's football team won the national championship. Yet Navy players were strictly amateur athletes at a time when some of the country's top college teams were semi-professional. As though to commemorate the undefeated season, Navy men stood with bared heads to hear for the first time the new official song, "Navy Blue and Gold."

Joseph W. Crosley, Chapel organist, wrote the score and Lieutenant Roy de S. Horn, Class of 1915, wrote the first two verses. The hymn begins:

> *Now, college men from sea to sea*
> *May sing of colors true;*
> *But who has better right than we*
> *To hoist a symbol hue?*
> *For sailor men in battle fair,*
> *Since fighting days of old,*

Have proved the sailor's right to wear
The Navy Blue and Gold.

Everyone connected with the Navy, ashore and afloat, felt great pride in the Academy teams. At ports all over the world ships of the Fleet listened in every Saturday during football season. Now half a million people try to buy tickets to the Army-Navy game. For the Naval Academy this brings a value beyond prestige and publicity: sale of football tickets produces up to eighty-five percent of the budget of the Naval Academy Athletic Association.

Nineteen other sports are financed by football gate receipts which also pay for such additional expenses as equipment, athletic facilities, and the yearly transportation of the Brigade and band to out-of-town games. The Army-Navy classic alone requires ninety buses to transport midshipmen from Annapolis to Baltimore and four fifteen-car trains from there to Municipal Stadium in Philadelphia.

From the standpoint of Academy training, the most important contribution of the football gate receipts has come to be the support of the Brigade's 24-sport intramural program. Not every midshipman can make a Navy team, yet every one must participate in one sport in each of the three seasons. The beginner is placed with men having about the same skill. The purpose is recreation, physical development and development of such traits as self-assurance, courage, determination and the competitive spirit. Those are qualities needed in a naval officer.

After World War II the Academy Sports Program paid more attention than ever to individual physical fitness. Torpedoings, air crashes and amphibious warfare had shown that survival depended on an officer's being in top shape.

Today midshipmen cannot graduate until they have passed agility tests during each of the first three years. There are nineteen obstacles in the tests that call for the use of many different muscles.

As might be expected, swimming requirements are strict. Plebes start in the shallow instruction pool. Before the end of the year they must be able to swim 100 yards without stopping and show that they have mastered the four standard strokes. In Youngster year they are required to swim 160 yards in four minutes. Second Classmen qualify in the 150-foot pool of the Natatorium by swimming a minimum of about a quarter mile. Drill in swimming ends this year, after the midshipman has made a jump from a height of 25 feet and has passed the test of swimming 20 yards under water.

In many ways future officers are taught to defend themselves. In the old days midshipmen learned to use broadswords, boarding pikes and cutlasses. Today they learn judo, wrestling and boxing. For years the Naval Academy boxing program has been outstanding.

To more than 20,000 Academy graduates the word boxing immediately brings to mind Spike Webb, the kindly, wise and courageous little boxing coach who held forth at the Yard for thirty-five years. To all former midshipmen Spike was more than a coach, friend and advisor —he was a part of the Academy.

Spike was born in a rough and poor section of Baltimore where he soon started fighting and lost his given name, Hamilton Murrell. He picked up "Spike" (from a steel shipboard tool, the marlinspike) because he hit so hard. But he stood only five feet, four and a half inches, weighing 135 pounds.

After more than one hundred professional bouts Spike went to France during the first World War to instruct American troops. While there he gave pointers to the fighting Marine,

Gene Tunney, who defeated Jack Dempsey for the world's heavyweight boxing championship. After the war Spike came to Annapolis.

From Navy Juniors to First Classmen, Spike was an inspiration. He had an uncanny knack for making boxers do their best. "Everyone is different," said Spike, "like thumb prints. A coach has to figure out how to get his ideas inside a boy's skull."

Spike could usually figure things out. When midshipmen were still engaged in intercollegiate boxing, no Academy team suffered a single defeat through eleven consecutive years. During his Academy days Spike also coached four U.S. Olympic Teams, another record. And whenever he traveled, some time was always spent around gyms where he liked to help out underprivileged kids.

Among thousands of letters pasted in scrapbooks are many which call him the greatest of boxing coaches. One especially would seem to bear this out. It came from a boy who had just won the Golden Gloves:

> Thank you, Spike, for helping a poor Negro boy make good.
>
> WALKER SMITH

Walker changed his name to Sugar Ray Robinson, often called the greatest fighter—pound for pound—in ring history.

The tales told about Spike Webb are legion. Among other things he was a great practical joker. Once he tried to get the football team "fighting mad" so they would defeat the Fighting Irish of Notre Dame. Just before the game he painted Bill, the Goat, a bright green.

In 1954 Spike retired. Two hundred officers gathered at a farewell banquet. One of his "boys"—Admiral Halsey—expressed the good wishes of all hands in a wire:

The Naval Academy will not be the same without you.

After retiring Spike stayed on in the home town he loved. As he approached seventy years of age, mail reached him addressed simply to: "Spike Webb, Annapolis, Md." In 1958 Spike remained a familiar figure as he strolled about town or the Yard, hat brim pulled down to eye level. That year another of Spike's "boys," Captain Slade D. Cutter, Director of Athletics, remembered the old coach who had helped him go undefeated through twenty-two collegiate heavyweight fights.

Captain Cutter, a letter man in boxing and football, made arrangements to have Spike's name inscribed on a seat in the new Navy-Marine Corps Memorial Stadium. The tribute was more than an individual gesture—all Navy men would want to see Spike Webb stick around.

The new stadium in West Annapolis was made possible by contributions from within and outside the Navy. Much of the help in building the 30,000-seat stadium came from young people who continue to send the Academy small sums for its support. The Congress is prohibited by law to underwrite such a project which is also too ambitious even for the Athletic Association to carry. Memorial Stadium is another landmark of the growth achieved since the days when Admiral Porter gave the first orders to convert Fort Severn into a gymnasium.

To insure smooth operation of intercollegiate sports, many extracurricular activities have been developed. Three committees take care of putting on contests. Arrangements must be made for pep rallies and team send-offs. For the Army game posters are put up and *Tecumseh* is painted. A Public Relations Committee stands by to brief the press, radio and television. The

Reception Committee sees that first-rate hospitality is provided for visiting teams.

In addition to sports about forty extracurricular activities have been developed for midshipmen who have interests outside of athletics. These organizations range from brigade and upper class administrative committees to hobby clubs and publications. Civilians are amazed that midshipmen with only Wednesday afternoons and Sunday evenings at their disposal can find time to work so extensively in these activities.

Midshipmen clubs are hard-working organizations. For example, midshipmen do all the programming and engineering connected with their broadcasts to Bancroft Hall from radio station WRNV. And their short-wave station, W3ADO, is known to "hams" all over the world.

Members of the Boat Club are allowed more time since this activity ties in with classes in seamanship and navigation. Sailing takes a great deal of time even in the twelve yawls and thirty sloops that cruise on Chesapeake Bay. In addition there are offshore races in big Academy yachts to points as far away as Bermuda.

Among the popular extracurricular events are the hops, or Naval Academy dances, when midshipmen invite their drags, or dates, from far and near. Committees arrange for numerous week-end dances as well as the big hops at Christmas and Thanksgiving and the Farewell Ball and Ring Dance at Commencement.

Until very recently Plebes could come to the hops only as spectators. Now they have six "Tea Fights," as the Fourth Class Informal Dances are called. These informal dances are held on Sunday afternoons.

About 400 girls are invited to each dance from a carefully screened Washington-Baltimore area list. On hand are 700 Plebes; hence the return of the unpopular stag line. Plebes are warned not to congregate in corners and to concentrate on their social graces rather than the punch bowl. Dancing with one girl all afternoon is frowned upon.

Some Plebes suspect that the Fourth Class dance is only partly for their pleasure. They see it being used as a wedge to break up the popular practice of "going steady."

Midshipmen with a flare for writing and art can try out for one of several publications. Through the years *The Log*, a biweekly, and its alternate week "son," *The Splinter*, have reflected life at the Academy. These carry news stories, jokes, cartoons and biographical sketches that stamp the times.

One hundred years ago midshipman humor often compared the actual hardships of naval life with the romantic misconceptions of civilians. Today, the high cost of living is the basis for many jokes such as this one in a 1958 issue of *The Splinter:*

> The author of a famous book on economics received a phone call one night. The voice said: "I question your statistics on the high cost of living today. My wife and I eat everything our hearts desire and we get it for exactly 68 cents a week."

> "Did you say 68 cents a week?" echoed the economist. "Could you speak a little louder?"

> "Yes," said the voice. "I did say 68 cents a week, but I can't speak any louder, I'm a goldfish."

More sophisticated material appears every six weeks in *Trident,* the professional magazine of the Brigade. Midshipmen who started writing for *Trident* have continued through their careers in the Navy to have articles published in national periodicals and in the *Naval Institute Proceedings*. This is now the world's outstanding magazine covering naval affairs.

IX

Sea Fighters From Annapolis

With the shocking news of the Japanese attack
on the Fleet at Pearl Harbor on Sunday, December 7, 1941, Naval Academy life received
the biggest shake-up experienced since the Civil
War. For the fifth time in less than 100 years
midshipmen entered a wartime regime. Athletics and other extracurricular activities became

secondary to extra study as the course was reduced to three years.

At the outbreak of World War II the ranking admirals of the Navy were men who had graduated from the Academy in the opening years of the century. Through the Fleet every class was represented down to new ensigns commissioned ahead of time the month war started.

Officers from Annapolis saw action in more than fifty theaters of operation. Hundreds of Academy men were cited for heroism, and most of the decorations worn today came from the global war or its aftermath at Korea.

In no other armed service is it so difficult to single out individual heroes as in the Navy where teamwork is a tradition. Aboard ship— from aircraft carrier to PT boat—every man has a duty to perform and every ship is a complete unit. In sea war there are no safe, rear-area headquarters; admirals are as close to death as seamen second class.

The few officers mentioned in this book would have been the first ones to describe their deeds as no more than standard performance for an American naval officer.

After knocking out most of the U.S. Pacific Fleet, the Imperial Japanese Navy swept through the Asian seas to cover troop landings as far south as Singapore. When American task forces opposed them in Bismarck Sea, they were consolidating the huge gain before a proposed conquest of Australia.

Lieutenant Edward "Butch" O'Hare, Class of 1937 and a graduate of Pensacola three years later, was one of the pilots who took off from the flight deck of the *Lexington* when the carrier came under attack by Mitsubishi dive bombers. He helped beat off the squadron and started in to refuel when another wave of nine Japanese planes were picked up at 12,000 feet, ten miles away.

Alone, with fuel and ammunition low, O'Hare banked to meet the enemy. His plane hurtled past the left flank of the formation; one Jap screeched down in smoke. He bagged another coming back on the right side. Out of the corner of one eye he saw the zigzag wake of the desperate *Lexington*.

Ragged holes began to show in the wings and fusilage of O'Hare's plane as he knocked down a third and fourth enemy bomber. Ammunition was almost used up when a fifth Jap burst into flames. But the remains of the attacking squadron pressed in. O'Hare roared into the barrage of the *Lexington's* anti-aircraft fire to cripple a sixth bomber. The ship was saved.

The citation that accompanied Butch O'Hare's Medal of Honor called his fight "one of the most daring, if not the most daring action in the history of combat aviation." The brave young officer continued in the spectacular carrier warfare until his number finally came up in 1945. He was reported missing in action off Tarawa.

The *Lexington* engagement was a prelude to the Battle of the Coral Sea when a new type of sea fight was recorded in naval annals—action in which opposing ships were miles apart.

In the Coral Sea—between Australia and the Solomon Islands—a classmate of O'Hare at Pensacola distinguished himself. This was Lieutenant John J. Powers who led an attack section of Dauntless dive bombers from the carrier *Yorktown*. On May 7, 1942, Powers located the enemy 170 miles away and led his group in through a heavy ack-ack screen. At the last possible moment he released his bomb and pulled out. Observers reported a tremendous explosion.

The next morning Powers sighted a big Japanese carrier from 18,000 feet. He led his men into the thick of the defensive fire after getting past the enemy's fighters. Other planes in the section dropped their bombs and pulled out, but Powers dove down and down. At two hundred feet he finally released to score a direct hit. When last seen, Lieutenant Powers' plane was being ripped to shreds.

The heroism of Lieutenants O'Hare and Powers became part of a new tradition for Navy pilots. Fighter and bomber groups chalked up astonishing records as new fast carriers were launched to check and then destroy the enemy.

Air Group 15, known as the "Fabled Fifteen," knocked out 650 Japanese planes and crippled 400 others in addition to being in on the sinking of about forty big ships.

Leader of the "Fabled Fifteen" was Commander David McCampbell, who became the Navy's high-scoring pilot with a total of thirty-four airborne enemy planes destroyed during a single tour of duty.

McCampbell of Bessemer, Alabama, graduated from the Academy in 1933. While a midshipman he qualified as an expert rifleman. In his First Class year he won the Eastern Intercollegiate Diving Championship. Before joining Admiral Mitscher's Task Force 58, where he made his record, McCampbell fought in scattered actions to keep open supply lines to Guadalcanal. That was later in 1942 when American naval forces first engaged the Japanese in ship-to-ship battles which saved our Army and Marine Corps fighters ashore.

The Battle of Guadalcanal on the high jungle island in the Solomons was the first of a long bloody series leading up to Iwo Jima and Okinawa off the home islands of Japan. The first U. S. troops on Guadalcanal were landed to oust 30,000 enemy defenders. By November,

1942, they were hard pressed by the Japanese. Admiral Halsey ordered five cruisers and eight destroyers to move up and cover the landing of fresh troops and supplies. The Japanese got reinforcements too—two battleships, a cruiser and fourteen destroyers—and moved down "the slot" of the Solomon Islands.

The battle opened in the air. American planes and anti-aircraft guns shot down about twenty-five Japanese bombers and torpedo planes. One of the disabled planes, ablaze and smoking, made a suicide dive into the superstructure of the cruiser *San Francisco*. Burning gasoline killed thirty of the crew.

At midnight, with no moon, the *San Francisco* led the cruisers and destroyers up Lengo Channel. Rear Admiral Daniel J. Callaghan radioed from the flagship: "We want the big ones!"

Out of the darkness came sudden stabs of light from the Japanese ships to pinpoint the

San Francisco. The cruiser received a terrible battering from the Japanese battleship *Hiei.* The fire was returned. In the next few minutes the sea between Guadalcanal and Savo Island lit up with gun flashes, tracers and the splashes of color that identified the hits of individual ships. In the din of battle few could tell Japanese vessels from American.

Japanese heavy guns concentrated on the *San Francisco.* Numerous hits were scored on the bridge and conning tower. Then a salvo killed Admiral Callaghan, all of his staff, the skipper and other officers and enlisted men. The command passed to Lieutenant Commander Bruce McCandless, ranking officer among the survivors.

McCandless had been knocked unconscious by the damaging salvo, but his head cleared quickly. He was barking out orders as he pulled himself to his feet on the hot, twisted deck.

The *San Francisco* scored her share of the eighty hits that finished the *Hiei,* then led the surviving American ships to safety.

The young Commander received the Medal of Honor and went on to become rear admiral. Calmness under fire and the will to fight back were traits recognized and developed in Mc-Candless, first as a Navy Junior and later as midshipman. He had been one of Spike Webb's most promising boxers.

The Battle of Guadalcanal lasted only twenty-four minutes, but it was one of the most furious in naval history. Only two destroyers of the American force escaped damage. Although Japanese ships suffered less, they scurried off to concede defeat. Never again did their surface units threaten Guadalcanal.

The costly fighting on that famous island marked the beginning of modern amphibious warfare—the taking of beachheads by troops carried from ship-to-shore in landing craft under enemy fire. The man who trained the first Marines to land on Guadalcanal was a member of the Class of 1912, Daniel E. Barbey, who as an admiral later commanded amphibious forces in the Southwest Pacific. To the men serving under him he was "Uncle Dan, the Amphibious Man."

Amphibious warfare brought a strange collection of ships into the Navy. The first one—with "Uncle Dan" aboard—was demonstrated in Washington. It was a barge equipped with wheel tracks from a tank. After bumping down Fourteenth Street, it shifted from automobile to boat for a crossing of the Potomac. Even on the demonstration trip it met with opposition, for all hands on the thing were arrested when they landed on the opposite bank. This was a wild waterfowl sanctuary, and Uncle Dan and his men were guilty of "unauthorized invasion."

From Guadalcanal to Okinawa, and from Africa to France, amphibious forces stormed the beaches in craft that improved with each costly landing. The boats grew in size until LSDs (Landing Ship, Docks) could carry more than 500 men.

The techniques learned under fire in World War II and the Korean War are taught today when Second Classmen arrive in the summer at Little Creek, Virginia, for indoctrination at the Navy's Amphibious Base.

The two-week program begins with movies filmed in the Pacific and European theaters during the 1940s. Next, midshipmen are taught to lower LCVPs (Landing Craft, Vehicles, Personnel) from an attack transport. They then learn to scramble down nets into the craft and finally "hit the beach" under simulated combat conditions.

Amphibious training also teaches midshipmen about the work of Navy frogmen. These daring amphibious troops were first used in World War II. Their job was to clear beaches of explosives and other underwater obstructions before the landing craft came in.

Movies and the talks of men who hit the beaches give some idea of the horrors encountered by troops who fought in the last two wars. There was more to the nightmare of landings than lowering barges in heavy weather and darkness, or in braving the barrage of fire on the open shore.

Inaccurate charts sometimes caused LSTs to be hung up helplessly on reefs while men were butchered from hidden gun emplacements. Heavy surf capsized other landing craft. Men who escaped being drowned by the weight of heavy packs staggered onto strange beaches nearly exhausted. Knife and bayonet attacks killed many; so did land mines and snipers. Amphibious landings could be as personally hazardous as the boarding of olden days.

Many Japanese-held islands between the Philippines and the Aleutians were forced to surrender when the defenders faced starvation or ran out of ammunition. The biggest single factor in cutting enemy supply lines was the Navy's submarine service.

Annapolis graduates who later attended submarine school at New London, Connecticut, commanded the underseas fleet that sank more than a thousand Japanese ships. At the start of the war, U.S. submarine crews were faced with a grave morale and safety problem: the new type torpedoes turned out to be mostly duds. Many a direct hit did nothing more than warn the enemy. But once operative the American submarines—always named after fish—accounted for six million tons of enemy shipping. On special missions the submarines evacuated high-ranking officers, photographed enemy harbors, transported gold and documents and brought supplies to guerilla allies.

A successful submarine officer could stand

confinement, physical hardship and almost constant danger. He also needed luck, and when that ran out only his great bravery remained. Many Annapolis men qualified. One of them was Commander Howard Walter Gilmore of Selma, Alabama, who graduated from the Academy in 1926.

Commander Gilmore took over the submarine *Growler* early in the war. In the summer of 1942 he earned the Navy Cross for sinking two Japanese destroyers and damaging a third as they lay at anchor in one of the protected ports. On another war patrol the *Growler* sank 25,946 tons of Japanese merchant shipping for which Commander Gilmore received a Gold Star in lieu of a second Navy Cross.

The *Growler* went on her fourth patrol in early 1943 and struck again. This time her skipper earned the Medal of Honor posthumously. The American submarine sank a freighter, damaged another, then sank two gunboats and rammed a third. The last part of Commander Gilmore's citation read:

> In the terrific fire of the sinking gunboat's heavy machine guns, Commander Gilmore calmly gave the order to clear the bridge, and refusing safety for himself, remained on deck while his men preceded him below. Struck down by the fusillade of bullets and having done his utmost against the enemy, in his final living moments Commander Gilmore gave his last order to the Officer of the Deck: "Take her down!"

"The submarines beat Japan," according to Admiral Raymond A. Spruance, who commanded fast battleships and was known in the Pacific as "the thinking machine."

Among the many who agreed with this opinion was Admiral Chester W. Nimitz of Texas,

Commander in Chief of the Pacific Fleet and an old submariner.

Admiral Nimitz was the planning genius of the Pacific war, which entered a crucial stage in October, 1944. Today Plebes often hear the name Nimitz for the first time in connection with the Admiral's often-quoted explanation of why a battleship is called "she." (Because she uses so much paint and powder.) History remembers his many important decisions. One of these was the appointment of Admiral Thomas C. Kincaid to command the Southwest Pacific Forces for the October invasion to reoccupy the Philippines.

Kincaid was born in New Hampshire, the son of an admiral. When he was sixteen, he received his Academy appointment from President Teddy Roosevelt. As a midshipman he played football and rowed on the crew. At graduation in 1908, *The Lucky Bag* described him as a "black-eyed,

rosy-cheeked, noisy Irishman." Thirty-three
years later newspaper reporters found the tall
officer with bushy eyebrows to be dignified, soft-
spoken and publicity shy. They were surprised
to learn that he had a full-rigged ship tattooed
on his chest.

Admiral Kincaid's forces—mostly small carriers (baby flat-tops) and PT boats—bore the
brunt of the Battle of Leyte Gulf in October,
1944. The Japanese went all out in this fierce
naval action, which was the biggest ever fought.
They were determined to smash the 600 transports which had landed MacArthur's troops and
to wipe out American warships. Instead, the
power of Japan's Navy was destroyed.

In the Battle of Leyte Gulf the Japanese first
used their *kamikazes,* or suicide planes, and lost
722 of them. The score for the gargantuan sea
fight showed the Japanese with a loss of sixty-
eight combat ships against twenty-one for the

U.S. Navy. About 7,000 Japanese planes were lost to 967 American.

Most Academy men saw action in the Pacific where the United States fought single-handed except for slight help from Australia and the Dutch. Officers in the European theater served at the invasions of Africa, Italy and France or were assigned to escort duty on the Atlantic convoys.

The whole vast, complex naval operation was under Fleet Admiral Ernest J. King, the man who had seen Spanish-American War action as a midshipman on summer assignment to the Fleet.

For the administrative job he did Admiral King was considered by many to rank with the great naval figures of the past. Never before had an Admiral been given command of so large an armada—2,000 big ships and other craft that totaled 100,000, together with 3,000,000 personnel.

Under Admiral King the Navy developed and used radically new weapons and methods. These were brought into use by the fast carriers and attack transports at Korea five years after the Japanese and Germans surrendered in 1945.

World War II also brought to the fore a new type of naval officer—one who, by the time he reached high rank, was a combination of sailor, engineer, military man, diplomat and scientist. Typical of the ideal to be attained by an Academy graduate was Admiral Arleigh A. Burke of Boulder, Colorado, Class of 1923.

A destroyer man, Burke commanded the famous Squadron 23—the "Little Beavers"—which fought twenty-two engagements in four months of World War II. He earned the nickname "31-Knot Burke" for the way he drove his destroyers just under boiler-bursting speed.

In addition to being a fighter, Burke held a

master's degree in science and engineering. He went on to flag command, and in 1955 took over as Chief of Naval Operations.

Admiral Burke and other World War II officers were in on the first use of the atomic bomb which wiped out almost 100,000 persons at Hiroshima on August 6, 1945. As a result the Japanese sued for peace in the costly war they had started.

In October, 1945, one month after peace was made in Tokyo Bay aboard the *Missouri*, the Naval Academy celebrated its centennial.

Three special platoons of midshipmen marched in uniforms of the past. The parade of Annapolis history showed the first acting midshipmen of 1845, dressed in blue jackets, vests and pantaloons. They were followed by cadet midshipmen of 1870, whose high collars featured crossed anchors. The platoon of 1900 naval cadets wore neat-fitting jackets with flaring rows of gold buttons; on their sleeves were the first stripes worn to show undergraduate ranks.

The combined classes of those early years had sent only 132 Academy men into the Fleet. In June of the centennial year, 1,046 ensigns were commissioned from the Class of 1946. They had attended the Academy only three years because of the customary wartime speed-up.

A memorial chapel service on October 7th honored the 729 graduates who had died in line of duty between the time when Commander Buchanan opened the school at Fort Severn until the end of World War II.

Heroes of Annapolis were given permanent memorials in the form of plaques which designated rooms in Bancroft Hall as Medal of Honor rooms—named after the famous graduates who had earned that citation.

X

June Week

After every war, the United States had cut back its Navy. But events following World War II were alarming. Naval action in the waters off Korea and the growing strength of Soviet Russia's Fleet brought plans for the expansion of the Naval Academy.

The Superintendent's Five-Year Plan was in effect by 1958 when sixty new acres of dredged

artificial land began to extend the Yard sea-
ward. Dewey Basin disappeared, and Farragut
Field pushed out into the Bay of Annapolis.
Architects' plans for a new academic building
and two more wings for Bancroft Hall were
approved. The huge Field House—with a capac-
ity of 15,000 persons—was completed, and work
started on the Navy-Marine Corps Memorial
Stadium.

The landfill project brought an end to the
career of the old Spanish man-of-war, *Reina
Mercedes*, which had been a station ship for
forty-five years. Midshipmen in the future will
miss the joke about the *Reina* being the "fastest
ship in the Navy"—from her having been made
fast to the pier for so long.

With expanded facilities have come new techniques of instruction and the most modern kinds
of equipment. In days gone by the changes at
sea were measured by centuries. An officer who
served under Christopher Columbus in the *Santa*

Maria would not have experienced too much trouble if he came aboard the *Constitution* 300 years later. But in only the last fifteen years the U.S. Navy has added one thousand new skills and job codes to sea fighting.

Leadership and command have become more important than ever in new ensigns. The streamlined fleet is geared to a type of warfare that will place heavy demands on officers expected to make rapid decisions.

The opportunity for leadership is now an established part of First Class Year. Midshipman officers, selected by aptitude, conduct and academic standings, administer the Brigade. These First Classmen hold ranks from Brigade Commander (also called Midshipman Captain) down to Platoon Sub-commander. The top man, known as the "Six Striper," wears six thin gold braid stripes on each sleeve; the lowest ranking First Classmen wear only one stripe. So that as many First Classmen as possible can assume command positions, the sets of officers change three times during the year.

A midshipman's final lesson in leadership and command comes during his last week at the Academy—June Week. In advance of graduation the First Classman's restrictions are lifted. He gets to know at first hand the meaning of R.H.I.P.—*Rank hath its privileges.*

The proud parents and sweethearts of First Classmen crowd the hotels at Annapolis for June Week events. Midshipmen in their white summer uniforms pass through the gates to mingle with the visitors.

The scene of June Week gaiety has been repeated more than one hundred times. Except for neon signs, plate-glass store fronts, and the wires and signs that have come with telephones, electricity and automobiles, Annapolis is little changed from Colonial times. The State House —where General Washington resigned as commander in chief—is still in use, for Annapolis is the capital of Maryland. Narrow old streets lead into two circles which remain in the heart of town. The English names of streets—King George, Prince George and Duke of Gloucester —recall the first settlement of 1634.

On the first Saturday in June, graduation events get under way with a dress parade on Worden Field in the forenoon. The end of that day is marked by the Ring Dance, so called because the Second Classmen put on their class rings for the first time. By the end of June Week they will be First Classmen.

Through the years the class ring ceremony has become a big event. Years ago it was the custom to throw the new owners into Dewey Basin. After Midshipman Leicester Smith was drowned in 1924, the dunking was replaced by the Ring Dance. At the end of the hop a midshipman's girl puts the ring on the third finger of his left hand after dipping it into separate binnacles of sea water which are sent by ships operating in each of the seven seas. The couple then walk through a big gilded replica of the ring.

The last religious service at the Academy for First Classmen is held the next day, which is known as "Sob Sunday." That name is carried on without any of the bitterness that marked its start—when insubordination ruined graduation exercises in 1883. Because of the large size of graduating classes, the Baccalaureate is held in the Field House instead of the Chapel to accommodate First Classmen and their families and friends.

Hops, parades, concerts and the Superintendent's Garden Party are a few of the events that follow in a hectic five-day period. There are also demonstrations on the Severn, in the air and at the Field House. Honors and awards are presented at special ceremonies; the Masqueraders put on a musical; the crew and tennis teams compete with West Point or some major college. The high pitch of excitement in the Yard is enough to make up for the year of hard work.

Late Tuesday afternoon parents and visitors fill the grandstands at Worden Field to witness the Presentation of Colors Parade. On this occasion the national flag and brigade flags are transferred from the old to the new color guard.

Each year the color guard is selected from midshipmen in the company which has won the year-long inter-company competition. Twenty-four companies vie for the honor. Academic grades, intramural sports, and excellence on the drill field add to a company's points. The company with the highest number of points wins the honor of carrying the official flags of the Brigade at all drills and parades. The company captain names the Color Girl who makes the actual presentation.

Just before 1730 (5:30 P.M.) of the great day, martial music can be heard as the Naval

Academy band comes on the field behind the Brigade Staff. Then the first column of companies swings in sight, marching in perfect step.

The Brigade forms in line of battalions and the music stops. After the national anthem is played, the midshipman captain directs the adjutant to "receive reports of the two Regiments."

Receiving the reports is an old Academy tradition. It uses a standard military formula to announce the year of the next graduating class. If the Class of 1963 is due to graduate, the Commander of the First Regiment flashes a sword salute and calls out:

"*Nineteen* men absent, sir!"

The Commander of the Second Regiment replies:

"*Sixty-three* men absent, sir!"

After the First Class has made this farewell gesture to its successor, the call comes for presentation of the colors. The old color guard and the new color guard—four men each, selected for top performance in athletics and professional subjects—face each other. Then the "Color Girl" and her midshipman escort present the flags to the incoming color guard.

With the order "Pass in Review!" the band strikes up "Anchors Aweigh," and the Brigade marches down the field past the reviewing stand.

Excitement continues to run high after presentation of colors, for that night the Farewell Ball, or June Ball, is held. First and Second Classes have their dance in Dahlgren Hall while the Plebes attend their first formal in Memorial and Smoke Halls with Third Classmen.

On Wednesday morning First Classmen report for breakfast formation for the last time. To commemorate the event they are allowed to appear in any uniform they choose. Once a midshipman took extreme advantage of this leniency. He not only selected pajamas as his "uniform" but had himself carried to formation in his bed by four Plebes.

Throughout the forenoon First Classmen say their final good-byes. The class will soon be scattered, and even roommates may not see each other for years. Midshipmen who have rated high in the Aptitude for Service system are most likely to rise in the Navy. This important evaluation of attitude, performance of duty, leadership and appearance usually indicates the average future. Another indication of future progress is the Superintendent's List made up of midshipmen who have stood high in studies, conduct and aptitude.

The changing tactics of naval warfare mean an even wider separation of classmates than in former years. Ten percent will go into the Marine Corps; others are headed for the Supply Corps, Construction Corps and other special branches. Until 1958, twenty-five percent of the graduates could volunteer for commissions in the Air Force, which at first had no academy with a four-year course.

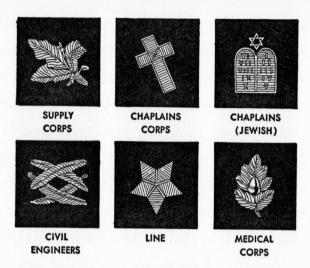

SUPPLY CORPS CHAPLAINS CORPS CHAPLAINS (JEWISH)

CIVIL ENGINEERS LINE MEDICAL CORPS

COMMISSIONED OFFICERS' DEVICES

Many of the First Classmen will maintain contact in the Fleet, for most of them will become "line" officers. In the General Line, assignments prepare them for command at sea.

Regardless of the branch a new ensign enters, his graduation establishes him as a "capable junior officer," which is part of the "Mission" of the Academy. After graduation from the Academy, the new officer takes with him a reminder

of the four years that made him capable—a copy
of *The Lucky Bag,* Naval Academy yearbook.

The Lucky Bag weighs about seven pounds
and measures twelve inches by nine with more
than 600 pages. In it are preserved memories
of Academy life: photographs of classmates;
highlights of events; pictures of officers and
civilian instructors.

Today the biographies of all First Classmen
appear in concise form, very different from the
college humor sketches of bygone years. But
The Lucky Bag retains the custom of recounting
the main events of the midshipman's life at
Annapolis in chronological order.

As a midshipman looks back over the "Deck
Log," he will recall incidents of Plebe Year with
its uncertainties and the abrupt change from
civilian life. Bits of nonsense will remain in his
mind for years, such as being required to memorize:

The latitude of Annapolis is 38° 58′ 53″ North
The longitude is 76° 29′ 08″ West

Visits in the homes of faculty members first made the Plebe feel some confidence. Then there was advice from the First Classman assigned to look after him.

After the trials of Fourth Class year, being a Youngster seemed like really living. The first summer cruise to foreign ports and a sample of life aboard ship filled him with enthusiasm for a naval career afloat. That year he became acquainted with the many ways a midshipman learns—or sometimes does not learn—to get around Regulations.

Memories evoked by *The Lucky Bag* include all sorts of devices to fool the Officer of the Watch. These included such tricks as smuggling food out of the mess hall or keeping pets in Bancroft Hall. Once a midshipman had a praying mantis tethered with a long piece of thread so it could be lowered out the window to feed on flies and grass. Another enterprising midshipman wired into the bell system in Bancroft Hall and was able to control the ringing of bells for reveille, meal formation and other activities.

In Second Class year most midshipmen remember the hardest work at the Academy. But with it were practical contacts: an exchange trip to West Point; amphibious warfare and aviation training; a greater awareness of what the Navy was doing abroad.

With First Class Year came the responsibilities of command within the Brigade and closer association with officers at the Academy. On Christmas leave 100 selected midshipmen took part in "Operation Information," a program of radio and television appearances. A First Classman was able to tell high school boys about opportunities at the Academy.

On the eve of graduation the First Classman's

MIDSHIPMAN SLEEVE RANK AND INSIGNIA

| 4TH CLASS | 3RD CLASS | 2ND CLASS | 1ST CLASS |

COMMISSIONED OFFICER INSIGNIA

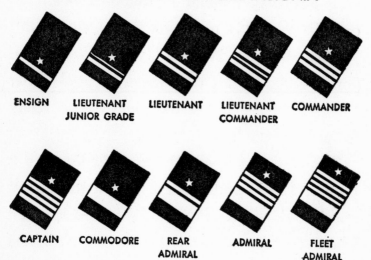

| ENSIGN | LIEUTENANT JUNIOR GRADE | LIEUTENANT | LIEUTENANT COMMANDER | COMMANDER |

| CAPTAIN | COMMODORE | REAR ADMIRAL | ADMIRAL | FLEET ADMIRAL |

thoughts center on the immediate future. His first billet as ensign will be tremendously important to his future. He may be thinking of getting married immediately as midshipmen have been able to do since June, 1942. And inevitably he will consider how to live on an ensign's annual base pay of $2,667.60. He will make more if he has a wife and draws subsistence and dependency allowances. And as an officer in the United States Navy he will have other advantages, including that of belonging to one of the world's most honored professions.

At 11:00 A.M. Wednesday, the last day of June Week, First Classmen are seated under the high arched roof of the Field House, ready to be graduated.

The chaplain opens the ceremonies with a prayer. The Superintendent says a few words and introduces the distinguished guest speaker. The tone of his talk is always serious to impress upon the midshipmen their great responsibility. They are not embarking on the business of seeing how much money they can make. Their job is to defend their country, which has always been the most noble of endeavors.

Soon after the awarding of diplomas begins, a note of humor enters the proceedings. Cheers rise from one section of the Field House and spread as a First Classman is lifted on the shoulders of friends. Grinning sheepishly he waves a blue and gold anchor. This is the "Anchor Man" of the graduating class, the man with the lowest academic rating. The entire Brigade rises to cheer. As midshipmen say of the Anchor Man who just made it: "There but for the grace of God walks a civilian."

The diploma means graduation with the degree Bachelor of Science. Then comes the administration of the oath that makes a midshipman an Ensign, U.S. Navy, and entitles him to one broad gold stripe on sleeves and shoulder bars. All hands join in the singing of "Navy Blue and Gold." This concludes graduation exercises, commissioning of new officers and the end of four years at Annapolis.

Once outside the Field House, the new ensigns have their shoulder bars adjusted by their mothers or sweethearts. For each new officer a naval career is about to begin.

When the excitement dies down, each young officer will have time to read the prized document he has received in the Field House. Its language of bygone days seems to give it great weight. The stirring words make graduates feel a part of something that is worthwhile beyond description:

> *Know ye, that reposing special Trust and Confidence in the Patriotism, Valour, Fidelity and Abilities of* ————, *I have nominated him and by and with the advice and consent of the Senate do appoint him an Ensign in the Navy.*
>
> *By the President.*

Index

LANDMARK BOOKS

WORLD LANDMARK BOOKS